Training the Versatile Hunting Dog

Chuck Johnson

photos by Blanche Johnson

Wilderness
Adventures
Press, Inc. ™

Belgrade, Montana

Dedication

This book is dedicated to our German wirehaired pointers, past and present.
Baron von Hohenzollern
Cody's Adventures
Hunhaven Duke
Hunhaven Annie Oakley
Hunhaven Belle Star
Hunhaven Hershey
Hunhaven Sprig
Hunhaven Silver Sage
Hunhaven Chukar
Dilli v. den drei Teufeln (Camas)

Chuck with Baron and Cody.

Table of Contents

Currently the North American Versatile Hunting Dog Association (NAVHDA) recognizes and maintains studbooks for the following breeds:

BI	Bracco Italiano	IS	Irish Setter
BA	Braque D'auvergne	LM	Large Munsterlander
BB	Braque Du Bourbonnais	PT	Pointer
BF	Braque Francais	PO	Portuguese Pointer
BS	Brittany	PP	Pudelpointer
CF	Cesky Fousek	SH	Slovensky Hrubosrsty Stavac
DP	Drentse Partridge	SM	Small Munsterlander
ES	English Setter	SP	Spinone
FP	French Spaniel	ST	Stichelhaar
GL	German Longhaired Pointer	VI	Vizsla
GS	German Shorthaired Pointer	WM	Weimaraner
GW	German Wirehaired Pointer	GR	Wirehaired Pointing Griffon
GO	Gordon Setter	WV	Wirehaired Vizsla
IR	Irish Red & White Setter		

Blanche and Baron on a pheasant hunt.

Chuck and Annie Oakley. photo by Brendt Phillips

Acknowledgements

Eleven years ago Dave Meisner, the founder of *Pointing Dog Journal*, asked me to become the Department Editor of The Versatile Hunting Dog column. I am grateful to Dave as well as to Steve and Jason Smith, my fine editors for the wonderful opportunity. *Pointing Dog Journal* is the only magazine that features a regular column on versatile hunting dogs. If you are not a subscriber, you need to sign up and get this outstanding magazine. There is a subscription form in the back of the book.

Over the years many dog trainers have shared their training techniques with me and I have shared that knowledge with the readers of PDJ. I want to thank them: Blaine Carter, John Crozier, Bob Farris, Jeff Funke, Ken Marsh, and others.

This book would not have been possible without the help of my wife and hunting partner, Blanche. We have hunted together for over forty years. Blanche is also a great photographer. She took most of the photos for this book and also edited it.

Finally, since this book has so much to do with our family of wirehairs, we also want to thank our daughters, Tracy and Jennifer, for the help they gave when they were still at home, in caring for our dogs and helping with the socialization of our puppies.

Chuck and Camas

Introduction

For the past 28 years Blanche and I have owned, bred, trained, and hunted German wirehaired pointers. We spend 50 days or more a year hunting both upland birds and waterfowl with our dogs. They are part of our family and live in the house with us. They also go to work with us every morning. Some of you might know me as the Versatile Hunting Dog Editor of the *Pointing Dog Journal*. For the last ten years, I have had the opportunity and the privilege of writing about versatile hunting dogs and working with Steve Smith and Jason Smith, the editors of the magazine.

Training the Versatile Hunting Dog is a book written for the amateur trainer and hunter. If you are interested in owning a dog that will hunt for you and will become part of your family as well as your hunting buddy, then this book will help you in training your dog. *Training the Versatile Hunting Dog* is different than any other training book. We will not only cover the training methods for hunting upland birds, but we also cover how to train your dog for waterfowl hunting and retrieving. The ability of your dog to track and retrieve wounded game is very important. We will show you how easy it is to train your dog to become an excellent tracker.

When you get your young puppy, he is eager to learn. He has no built-in fears and he is a sponge ready to soak up knowledge. The first sixteen weeks of his life are crucial in socializing him. This is the time for you and your family to establish your bond with him. Proper socialization will produce a dog that is emotionally sound. That is why it is important to choose a breeder who starts socializing his puppies shortly after birth, and why it is important for you to get your puppy no later than eight weeks of age.

The first year is also crucial in exposing your puppy to the hunting field. Most training books start with putting the controls on a young dog. Hunters are urged to get their dogs under control. We believe that it is important to let your dog have fun the first year. Let him learn on his own; get him into wild birds as much as possible. Let him make mistakes. He will learn by his mistakes and develop his full hunting potential. Using an electric collar and putting the controls on your dog in the first year will hinder his natural ability. Your dog will never reach his full hunting potential. In the first part of this book, we will show you how to give your young pup the opportunity to become a great hunting dog. Both you and your dog will have more fun and find more birds using our methods. At the end of the first season you will be thrilled at your dog's hunting ability and your hunting friends will be amazed at what a great hunting dog you have. The second hunting season is the time to whoa train and force break your dog after he has developed his inherited hunting traits. In the second part, we will show how to put the controls on your dog. By following these revolutionary methods, you will have a Brag Dog that will be the envy of other bird dog owners.

Let me give you an example. Our friend, Gary Popiel, bought a wirehair from us a few years ago and trained Patches using our methods. Gary stopped in at the end of the 2005 season to chat. He told me that Patches had over ten invitations to go hunting. Fortunately for Gary, Patches was allowed to bring along a friend: Gary. Gary's hunting friends have both pointers and Labs. However, they know that Patches will go into the high, tough cover and find pheasants better than their pointers, and she will retrieve ducks in cold water where their retrievers don't like to go. Gary smiled and said, "I get invited to hunt on some great ranches in Montana because of my dog. She is the best dog I have ever owned and she was the easiest to train. She practically trained herself. Patches is now nine. When you have your next litter, reserve a pup for me. I am sold on versatile gun dogs."

This fall as I was finishing this book, Blanche and I got a new female pup: a VDD Drahthaar we named Camas. We started hunting Camas on wild birds when she was sixteen weeks old. I have included a section on Camas and how she developed her hunting abilities using the same methods that I recommend in training your dog. I have also included stories and examples of a number of other versatile dog owners and how they have had success training their dogs using the methods in this book.

I suggest that you read the entire book before you start your training. Then you can go back and read the individual chapters again, as you are training your dog.

Chukar on point.

Do-It-All Dogs

"Blanche, we lost another duck!" The flock of bluebills had buzzed our water blind just at daybreak. We knew they wouldn't set down in the decoys, so we had stood up and fired as they passed in front.

We each had a duck on the water and both of them appeared to be dead, but we didn't have a versatile gun dog. So, now it was time to unload our guns, get out of the blind, uncover our johnboat, push it out into the water, start the motor, and retrieve our ducks. But by the time we got to where the ducks had fallen, there was only one duck. The other one had disappeared. We would have seen it if it had flown, so it must have either dived to the bottom and drowned, or escaped over to the reeds near the far shore. After a futile thirty-minute search, we gave up.

We were hunting the Missouri River between South Dakota and Nebraska. While there, we hunted ducks in the morning and pheasants and quail in the afternoon with our English pointer, Brandy. Brandy did a great job on upland birds, and he would occasionally retrieve a duck in the water for us. However, this was early November.

Ice was on the gunnels of the boat and the water temperature was dangerously low, so Brandy stayed home.

This was during the late 1970s, when we made annual hunting trips to South Dakota, where we always had good success on both ducks and upland birds. Unfortunately, we also lost a lot of ducks. What we needed was another dog to handle the waterfowl hunting. But we were in a bit of a conundrum because, even though we liked retrievers, we preferred hunting over pointing dogs.

We got our first dog, an English setter, the month after we were married. Six years later we got an English pointer. Both were good upland bird dogs. Brandy, our English pointer, would also retrieve ducks for us. However, his coat was not suited for cold-water duck hunting.

After that season, I read an article by Jerome Robinson, *"Drahthaar Uber Alles."* Robinson wrote about Adolph, a German wirehaired pointer owned by a man named Mack Ballard. In the article, Ballard claimed that Adolph could find more birds, hold them steadier, and retrieve more game on land and water than any other breed of dog. He also claimed to have hunted Adolph for ducks or upland birds in the morning, and geese in the afternoon. He even used Adolph to run rabbits and tree raccoons. Adolph was truly the do-it-all dog.

There was a picture of Adolph in the article. I had never seen a German wirehaired pointer before and was about to remark that they looked a little ugly, when Blanche observed that the dog's bushy mustache and eyebrows, grizzled with gray, made him look a lot like me. "Blanche," I said, "this is the dog for us!"

Another thing that impressed me was that Ballard had also claimed to have trained Adolph to distinguish between the boxes of crackers in his store. He would entertain his customers by telling Adolph to fetch either the round or the square box

Duke brings back a pheasant on the afternoon hunt.

of crackers. Adolph would always bring back the correct box. What a dog! I could see us now, after a successful hunt for pheasants and ducks, sitting in the clubhouse extolling the virtues of our versatile dog with our hunting buddies. "Fellas, it's time for some refreshments. What's your pleasure? Should we have the twelve-year-old or the eighteen-year-old Scotch tonight? Don't bother getting up - I'll have my dog fetch the correct bottle."

That summer we located a breeder of German wirehaired pointers and got our first pup, a dog we named Baron. The breeder suggested that we join the North American Versatile Hunting Dog Association (NAVHDA). Fortunately for us, there was a local chapter in our area that we subsequently joined. Our chapter had an active training program, and the more experienced members were very helpful in getting us started with our new puppy.

So again in October, we made our annual trip to South Dakota, and by this time four-month-old Baron was already pointing birds. We were hunting pheasant on the flatlands above the Missouri River. There was a large pond located in the middle of one of the fields where we hunted upland game. Baron loved sneaking up on the pond with us, as we tried to jump-shoot mallards. Whenever we killed a duck, he would jump in the water and retrieve it to shore. Still too small to carry the duck very far, he would drag it to us wagging his tail. Baron loved the morning hunts in the duck blind and soon learned to scan the skies, watching for incoming ducks. When we would stand up to shoot, Baron would hit the blind door, jump out of the blind, and wait for the ducks to hit the water. He even learned to give us dirty looks if we didn't bring down any birds.

That first year Baron needed some help retrieving wounded ducks, as he got tangled in the decoys several times. But he was an enthusiastic hunter, and we lost far fewer birds. We also used Baron back in Ohio as the main dog on our hunting preserve. Most hunters who didn't own a dog would ask us to use Baron when we guided for them. They knew that he had an uncanny ability to find birds. He learned to circle a pheasant and work back toward the hunters, effectively pinning the bird. Often, when a hunter would wing a bird, I would send Baron out to retrieve it. The hunters were always amazed at his ability to find even a slightly wounded bird.

Several years later, Blanche and I fell in love with Montana. We took a hunting trip to the Big Sky Country and found a bird hunter's paradise. Eastern Montana prairies have good populations of sharp-tailed grouse, Hungarian partridge, sage grouse, and pheasant. There are also a great many potholes and excellent waterfowl hunting. About the only thing Montana lacked was bird hunters; we could hunt all day and never see another hunter. By now we had an expanded family of four wirehairs: Baron and Cody, and Duke and Annie, their son and daughter.

Hunting the prairies required an adjustment for our dogs and us. Birds are spread out over vast grasslands, which require a lot of legwork in order to find birds. Being fast learners, our dogs soon learned to make large, looping casts, and discovered that Huns and sharptails will not allow a dog to pressure them. After flushing several coveys of birds because they tried to get too close to them, the dogs learned to point as soon as they scented birds. The ranches we hunted had stock ponds for cattle. During the fall migration, we would usually find ducks resting on these ponds. We would change shells from lead to steel and sneak up on the pond from two sides, hoping to surprise the ducks and get a shot. Each of us would take a dog. If we were successful, the dogs would retrieve the ducks, and we would then continue hunting upland birds.

Fall in Montana is a perfect time for a "cast and blast" trip. We have some of the finest blue ribbon trout streams in the country, and the rivers also have many small islands that hold pheasants. Our trips would start with a float down the river fly fishing for large trout. When we got to an island, we brought out our shotguns and dogs and hunted the brushy cover for birds. Duke, our big male, loved these trips. He would sit on the back seat of the boat and watch us fish, but when we would land on an island, he would be raring to go after birds. We would often find ducks at the end of an island. A good day's trip usually resulted in several trout caught and released and a couple of pheasants and ducks in the cooler.

Besides pointing and retrieving, tracking is an important attribute that all the versatile breeds possess. You never know when you will need to track down a wounded bird or game animal. Versatile breeds have been bred and trained to track both feather and fur. In Europe, hunting customs and laws are strict about recovering all the game that is shot. Here in America, where hunters and hunting are increasingly under attack, it is important that we do not waste game. When we shoot a bird and do not find it, we provide anti-hunters with ammunition to condemn hunting. Unfortunately, except for NAVHDA, the versatile breed clubs, and the JGV tests, there is very little training or emphasis on tracking and recovering game.

For the last 28 years, versatile gun dogs have been the center of our life. They are constant companions in the field and in our home. If you enjoy hunting both waterfowl and upland birds and you want a dog that can do it all and will make a great companion and friend of the family, any of the versatile gun dog breeds will fit your needs. I must confess to one shortcoming of the breed: I still haven't been able to train our wirehairs to distinguish between the twelve- and the eighteen-year-old bottles of scotch, but I am still working on it.

Chukar steady to flush.

Bridget Nielson's Vizsla Jake shows strong desire retreiving a duck. photo by Ellie Rock

What to Look for in a Versatile Dog

There are a number of qualities and abilities that you should look for when you are picking out your future dog. Versatile dogs make ideal family dogs. So the dog's temperament is vitally important. You want a dog that is emotionally stable. He should be friendly and like people, especially children. You want a pup that wags his tail and comes quickly to you when he sees you approach his kennel. I like a pup that is bold; one that likes to explore and is not afraid of his own shadow. You also want a pup that has intelligence. An intelligent pup will learn faster and be easier to train. Physical attributes are extremely important. In order for your dog to have the physical ability to hunt hard and well, he needs to have good conformation and good overall physical attributes.

Let's start with a sound bite and sound teeth. The ideal bite is a tight scissors bite; where the upper teeth come over the lower teeth. Eyes should be bright with no eyelid problems. Coats vary on versatile breeds. I personally prefer a short dense coat on the body of my wirehairs. I also like them to have a full beard. Coats are really a matter of personal preference. A longer softer coat will pick up more burrs and require more maintenance. Sound hips and legs are extremely important. If your dog has leg or hip problems he will not be able to hunt hard. He also will not be able to hunt as long, and he will become incapacitated before his time. Make sure that your breeder has had both the parents x-rayed and that the results are good. I prefer the Penn-HIP x-ray. It gives you a percentage of tightness instead of a more general ranking of good, fair, or poor. Look at the history of the breed line. Go back several generations. Make sure that this line is free of hip problems. The same caution applies to legs. Ask your breeder what, if any, leg problems he has experienced in his breeding program. Good sound feet are often overlooked. Your dog will be covering many miles on his feet and legs every time he hunts. I like to see a dog with good tough pads. If they feel like sand paper, they are tough and will be less likely to get sore or cut.

Young pup shows an intense point at 8 weeks.

You want to buy your versatile dog from a breeder who is breeding hunting dogs. The parents and grandparents of your pup should be hunting dogs. A dog's natural ability is extremely important. The first part of our book will cover each of the dog's natural abilities and how to develop them during his first year.

HERE ARE THE ABILITIES YOU SHOULD LOOK FOR IN YOUR PUP:

- **Good nose**: This is the single most important quality in a hunting dog.
- **Intense point**: There is no sight more thrilling than watching your dog intensely pointing a bird.
- **Strong desire**: A dog with a strong prey drive and desire will hunt hard and find a great many more birds than a dog with low desire.
- **Cooperation**: Cooperation and desire go hand in hand. It is a balancing act between the two. It is important that a hard-charging, high-desire dog be willing to work with you in the hunting field. You want him hunting for you, not self-hunting.
- **Search**: You want your dog to make a thorough search of the cover.
- **Stamina**: A dog with good stamina can hunt hard all day.
- **Retrieving ability**: Most versatile breeds love to retrieve. I usually force break all of my dogs after I have developed their natural ability. However, I want a dog that shows a love of retrieving as a puppy.
- **Love of the water**: One of the great advantages of owning and hunting a versatile dog is their love of hunting both upland birds and waterfowl. You want your pup to enjoy going into the water. As part of his job, he will be doing water retrieves for the ducks and geese you shoot during your waterfowl hunts.

These are the qualities that you want in your puppy. Most of these qualities your puppy will inherit from his parents, grandparents, and great grandparents. The genetic attributes that a pup receives from his ancestors are an extremely important part of his makeup. These inherent qualities make up at least 80% of your pup's total ability. They are the foundation blocks in your puppy's total package. The better his inherent qualities, the better your chances of having an outstanding hunting dog.

Love of water.

VC Aspen, Blane Carter, and new pup Ecco. photo by Patricia Carter

How to Select the Right Puppy:
Select the Right Breeder

Let's just say your current hunting dog is now getting on in years and it's time to look for a new puppy. You know what breed you want, but how do you determine who is the best breeder for you? The key to getting a good puppy is in picking a good breeder. If you select a quality breeder who has a successful training and testing program, and has a history of producing puppies that are well socialized and possess the natural characteristics that go into the make-up of a good hunting dog, then you have an excellent chance of getting the right puppy. Pick the breeder first, then the puppy. Good breeders do not sell dogs in the newspapers. Good breeders have developed a good reputation by producing quality dogs and hunting them on wild birds and using a good testing program.

Genetics, the inherent qualities that your puppy gets from his ancestors, are the single most important aspect of your dog's future hunting ability. In my opinion, 80% or more of your dog's natural ability is derived from his genes. Dogs with excellent bloodlines develop their hunting ability early and are much easier to train. If you are able to get your young dog out into the wild bird field and into wild birds they will almost train themselves. Our newest pup, Camas, is a great example. A good breeder will have a history of his breeding line and detailed test or trial records as well as a history of high-performance dogs going back generations.

TO LOCATE A GOOD BREEDER USE THESE SOURCES:

- **Referrals**: Talk to your hunting partners and people who have had a number of hunting dogs. They will most likely have several names of quality breeders.
- **Magazines**: Publications such as *Pointing Dog Journal* and *Gun Dog* often write articles about breeders.
- **Breed Clubs**: Breed clubs for the various breeds of dogs usually have a referral list of member breeders. Many of the versatile breed clubs have a series of hunting tests that a dog must successfully pass before it can be approved for breeding. Many of these clubs also have breed wardens and a breed test where all of the dog's physical characteristics are evaluated and scored. They also evaluate the dog's gait. There is a list of the breed clubs and their websites in the back of this book. The websites will give you a great deal of information about the breed philosophy and tests and member clubs. I recommend that you go to the website of the breed in which you are interested and see what they have to offer. Go to field events, tests, and trials. At these events you can meet a number of breeders and observe their dogs. You can also talk to a number of participants and get their opinions and references.
- **Local Sporting Dog Clubs**: Most areas of the country have local sporting dog clubs. Attend their work sessions and talk to their members.

Prospective owners visiting with pups.

Using these sources, you should have a list of several breeders that you want to contact. Next, compose a list of questions that you want to ask each breeder. Here are nine groups of questions that you should ask your prospective breeder before you put your money down for your new hunting puppy:

1. Does the breeder hunt? Find out what birds and how many days a year the breeder hunts his dogs. How old are the sire and dam of the litter of puppies that he has available? Does he hunt the sire and dam? What are their hunting ranges, and styles?

2. What program does the breeder have for testing and evaluating his line of dogs? A good breeder has a planned program that includes evaluation of his dogs by outside judges. You want to know what programs and tests a breeder uses to determine the success of his or her kennel and what proof do they have that their breeding program is successful. There are several good testing programs available. The various versatile dog organizations all have similar testing programs. One of the best is the North American Versatile Hunting Dog Association's (NAVHDA) Natural Ability Test. According to NAVHDA's handbook, "The Natural Ability Test measures seven hereditary characteristics that are fundamental to the makeup of a good, reliable hunting dog." Another good testing organization is the JGV.

There are three phases to the NAVHDA test: the Field Phase, the Tracking Phase, and the Water Phase. Puppies up to sixteen months of age are tested and evaluated for nose, search, water work, pointing, tracking, desire to work, and cooperation. Breeders who are active in NAVHDA encourage the buyers of their puppies to enter their puppies in the Natural Ability Test. These breeders are very interested in having as many of their puppies as possible tested. The Natural Ability Test is an excellent way for a prospective owner to judge the quality of puppies being produced by a breeder.

Even though their new owners are often the ones handling the puppies in the test, NAVHDA records and keeps the test results for every puppy that is tested, categorized by each breeder. You can obtain the test results, referred to as a "breeder's report", for each breeder at a nominal cost from NAVHDA, whose address is provided in the back of this book. These reports will show the test scores of all of the dogs produced by that breeder. If a breeder's test scores show a high number of young puppies passing the Natural Ability Test, it is a good indication that your breeder is producing good prospects. The breeder's report will also show you all of the pups from that breeder that did not pass the test. If you are looking for a certain characteristic in your dog, you can see the scores of these characteristics.

Let's say you do a great deal of waterfowl hunting. It is important that you get a pup that will excel in the water. The breeder's test scores will show you the results of the water work on each pup tested by that breeder. The natural ability results give the prospective dog buyer an indication of the natural traits that a puppy possesses. When you buy a puppy, you are looking for built-in characteristics and natural talent. A breeder who has a long history of his pups scoring well in Natural Ability is a better indication that you are going to get a pup that will turn into a good hunting dog, than a breeder who has a well-trained sire or dam with unproven offspring.

Copy of Pen Hip.

Copy of a NAVHDA pedigree.

The AKC also has a testing program, AKC Hunting Tests For Pointing Breeds, that is an aid in evaluating dogs. There are three tests: Junior Hunter, Senior Hunter, and Master Hunter.

No matter what test the breeder advocates, the important point is that the breeder has a program and tests his dogs. The tests will give you a good look at the various breeds of dogs and their performances. It will also give you a chance to meet and talk to many different breeders. Remember, often the successful breeders do not advertise on a regular basis. So you can gain some valuable, practical information on breeders from the people who are active in the various tests and programs.

3. How does the breeder socialize the pups in his litters? Socialization of a young puppy is extremely important. Make sure that quality time has been spent with all the pups in a litter before you get your new puppy.

4. Can the breeder you are talking to recommend other breeders of similar quality? The successful breeders normally have a waiting list of buyers, and if they have a sound, successful program, they usually are not afraid to recommend other quality breeders. Call the other breeders and inquire about the breeder in which you are interested. Other breeders are far better able to judge the quality of the kennel and pups being produced than a customer.

5. What positive qualities does the breeder like in his dogs? You can count on the breeder waxing eloquently about the superior quality of his breed, which is fine, because you will get a good idea of what qualities he has stressed in his breeding and training program. If these are the qualities you are looking for, then this is one indication that this might be the right breeder for you.

Pups should be introduced to birds and water at an early age.

6. What qualities does the breeder feel he needs to improve in his dogs? What problems has he experienced with his line of dogs? These problems might have to do with conformation, hip problems, fieldwork, retrieving, or any number of things. If a breeder tells you he has never experienced a problem of any kind, beware. A good breeding program is always a work-in-progress, and there is no such thing as a perfect dog. A top breeder, no matter how successful, is always trying to improve his breeding line; a good breeder will be happy to discuss with you the areas that he is working on to improve his line of dogs.

7. What guarantees does the breeder offer to buyers? This might be a touchy subject with some breeders, but most of the good breeders offer a guarantee. The minimum guarantee that you should expect is one that covers the health of the pup. You have the right to expect a sound, healthy pup: one with no genetic flaws, no hip problems, or any other physical problem that would inhibit the dog from hunting. Ask the breeder if he has his dogs tested for hip dysplasia. The two most popular tests for hips are OFA and Penn-HIP. Good breeders always test the sire and dam for hips before breeding. Also inquire as to whether the pups have had their vaccinations, been wormed, and have had their dew claws removed. A good breeder has confidence in his dogs and his breeding program. He does not want a person to have one of his dogs if the dog happens to be unsound or does not fit in with the owner's needs or expectations.

8. When will the next litter be available? If the breeder has answered all of the questions to your satisfaction, and you have decided that you want to buy a pup from him, ask him when his next litter will be available. Also ask him who the sire and dam will be. Have the breeder send you their registration papers showing their certified pedigrees. Most breeders have a brochure that features their kennel, complete with photos of their dogs and their breeding program. I also like to have a photo of the sire and dam. Many people like to visit the breeder and see his kennel operation before buying.

9. Finally, you need to tell the breeder what type of dog you want. Discuss with him how often and how hard you hunt, and what type of game birds you hunt most. If you are hunting the prairies, you probably want a fairly wide-ranging dog. If you are hunting the grouse covers of New England or the Midwest, you will want a closer-working dog. Do you want a hard-charging alpha-type dog? An alpha dog can be a handful to train and own. You want to match your personality and ability with the dog as much as possible. As an aside, one mistake that many dog buyers make is the false assumption that all female dogs are easier to handle. This is not always the case. In my line of wirehairs the males are more laid back and easier to handle than the females. Trust your breeder to help you select the pup that he feels is best suited to your needs.

Once you have qualified your breeder, it is certainly not necessary to visit the kennel to get a good pup. However, I find that I can make a better judgment of the kennel and the dogs with firsthand observation. As a breeder, I am also impressed with customers who take the time and spend the effort and money to visit my kennel. I want to make sure that all of my pups are going to find a good home with a person who likes dogs and will hunt the dog. A personal visit gives me an opportunity to size up a prospective customer. As a prospective buyer, you should be prepared for questions from the breeder about your hunting desires, and your past experience in owning and caring for dogs.

A good kennel and breeding program costs money. The initial price of your pup is the smallest part of your investment. Your dog food and vet bills over the next ten to fifteen years will far exceed the cost of the new puppy. So be prepared to pay a reasonable fee for a new pup. Also make sure you plan ahead, as many breeders have deposits up to a year or more in advance for their pups. Don't wait until six months or less before you start your search for a pup.

Asking intelligent questions, getting tests results, and dealing with a committed breeder will certainly improve your chances of getting a good puppy with the potential to become the hunting dog of your dreams.

A good breeder makes sure his or her puppies are well socialized.

Young pups take their first ride in the truck.

Setting up a Home for Your New Puppy

At this point, you have made a choice of what breed of dog you want, selected a breeder, put down a deposit, and are eagerly waiting the time when you can pick up your new puppy. Now is the time to get the equipment and supplies you will need to take proper care of your new pup. We strongly recommend that your pup be raised in your home. The notion that a real hunting dog must be a kennel dog is a myth. A dog that is raised in your home with you and your family is able to bond with you. He gets to know your voice and your body language. The better your dog knows you, the better it will respond to you. A dog that is raised with the family, and with at least some house time, usually becomes a confident, well-socialized animal.

Let's start with housing. Your puppy is going to need a place to sleep and a place of his own for quiet time. There are many different types of housing for dogs. Whatever option you choose, the following elements must be present. The doghouse must be dry, it must allow a dog to stay out of the heat during the summer, and it must be warm enough for your dog in the winter. If you have an outside kennel, make sure that part of the kennel run is shaded. Dogs cannot stand high heat. They will expire quickly when temperatures get into the nineties. I use the Scott dog kennels. They have a large doghouse and an enclosed and covered run for each dog, and they are fairly easy to assemble, with insulation that can be added for colder climates. They also have a metal dog feeder that can be attached to the inside of the run. You should also get a large plastic bucket for water and use a snap to attach it to the wire side so your dog does not spill it. It is important that your dog has plenty of fresh water each day. You can also build outdoor kennels. Many people will build kennel runs in their garage or in an outbuilding.

You will need a place for your hunting dog to get daily exercise. I built a six-foot chain link fence area around my Scott dog kennels. This gives my dogs an area of thirty feet by seventy feet in which to exercise. I also have my training table in the fenced area and do a lot of my training there. We do not recommend that you let your pup have the full run of the yard unattended. Bad habits and behavior, such as digging, can develop.

Young pups love to chew and they will be teething, so buy him his own toys. Large rawhide or synthetic bones are great toys. A good quality food is essential for your dog. Spend the money on one of the high quality dog foods; Iams, Eukanuba, or Purina all make high quality dog foods. They have research labs that have tested and developed quality foods. They have also added the essential vitamins and minerals that are necessary for a dog's health. All three of these companies have special foods for puppies. They offer puppy food for small, medium, and large dogs. Make sure that you pick the right food for your puppy. Ask your breeder or vet for their recommendation on food. You will need at least two dog bowls, one for food and one for water.

We firmly believe in having your pup spend time with the family in your house on a daily basis. The more the dog bonds with you, the easier it will be to train him. Bird hunting with a dog is a team sport; you and your dog must get to know and like each other and work together to be successful in the bird field. Having your pup as part of the family will help to establish this bond. Plus, dogs are a great joy to have around. No matter how tough the day goes for you, they are always happy to see you.

When your dog is in the house, you should have a dog crate for him. There are times when you want your dog to be quiet and the best way to accomplish that is to put him in a crate. He will also have times when he wants to be alone, and he will soon learn to go into his crate. This is his private area. If you have children in the house, they should be taught to leave pup alone when he is in his private space. I like the travel crates. They can not only be used in the house, but also can be put in the car and used when your dog travels with you.

It will take you several weeks to house train your young dog. There will be accidents on the floor. Most pet shops sell a liquid that will clean up accidents and take away the odor.

You will also need a dog collar and a dog lead.

Finally, you will need to prepare the family for the arrival of your new puppy. It is important that all of the family understand that a puppy needs food, water, and quiet time. If you have young children, make sure they understand not to tease or abuse the pup. Explain to them not to shoot smurf balls at the pup or use a cap gun around him. A young pup needs to be carefully introduced to loud sounds and to the gun.

Young dogs learn best and develop best when they have a routine. Puppies need to be fed two times a day. Set up definite feeding times and try to stick to them. Also, your puppy will need a series of shots. The breeder will have started giving the shots to your pup, and should give you a list of those shots. It is an excellent idea to take your new puppy to your vet the first week and have a check up. At that time the vet can go over what shots your pup will need and when.

I like to keep my first commands minimal. I teach my new pups *come, kennel, sit, go out,* and the most important command at that age, *NO*. Let your pup have fun. Give him time to get used to you and your family. Save the whoa training for later; after he has had a full season of hunting. The first year of your pup's life should be spent having fun, bonding with the family, and developing his desire and drive.

Every dog needs his special personal place.

Our grandson Charlie feeding our dogs.

Puppy Training and Socialization:
The First Eight Weeks

I started training my own bird dogs thirty years ago. There was always a great deal of excitement and anticipation when I brought home a new puppy. I read a large number of popular training books and found them, for the most part, to be too rigid, complete with formal training sessions and timetables for accomplishing certain elements of training, with very little fun thrown in. The pups and I got through the training sessions, but I always thought there had to be a way to improve on conventional training methods to build a better bond with my pup while having more fun doing it.

Like many of you, I've learned over the years that my dogs know a lot more about finding birds than I do. They have an infinitely better nose, and are born with the genetic traits to point, back, scent birds, and hunt. As trainers, our job is to give them the opportunity to develop their God-given talents to the fullest.

When our wirehair, Annie, had a litter of pups I decided to alter my training methods in hopes of creating a better bond with the pups, and to get them off to a great start in their lives as bird dogs. I kept three females from Annie's litter of six. At seven-months old, the pups had been taught the commands to *come, kennel,* and *fetch,* as well as to point, back, search, and retrieve. They were introduced to the gun at eight weeks of age and, by the time they were seven months old, had hunted sharptails, Huns, pheasants, prairie chickens, sage grouse, ducks, and geese in six states.

The great part about it is that we had fun. There were no formal training sessions, and I did not use a check cord or an electronic collar. My only equipment consisted of a whistle, a few training dummies, a blank pistol, and some pen-raised quail. We didn't have a timetable, because these pups learned while playing. When they were ready to learn a new command, I introduced the command during a play session. I firmly believe that you need to spend time bonding with your pup and giving him generous doses of love. If you develop a strong, loving bond he will do anything in the world to please you. So, let's get started. With encouragement, coaching, and a lot of love, we're going to develop a young pup into a fine bird dog and hunting partner and have fun doing it.

The important elements in the makeup of a successful hunting dog are genetics and proper socialization. Genetics and the inherent qualities in selective breeding of dogs produce puppies that have a good nose and a desire to hunt, point, and back. You cannot put these qualities into a dog; they either possess them at birth or they don't. Our job is to bring out these qualities, to help our puppies develop to their fullest potential.

The first sixteen weeks are the most important in a young dog's life. This is the critical period of socialization, when the pup develops relationships with other animals, people, and especially with its master. The quality and quantity of time you spend with your young pup will determine whether you have a friendly, happy pup that is self confident, bold, adventurous, and a pleasure to be around, or a pup that is shy and fearful of other people and animals.

Blanche and I start bonding with our pups at their birth. Annie delivered in the middle of the night, and as the pups were born, we helped clean them up. We picked them up, weighed them, and blew lightly in their faces. One of the first senses for a new pup is smell. Their ability to smell their mother is how they find their way to nurse. By breathing on the newborns, we were establishing a bond with them, similar to the one their mother establishes with them at birth. During the first few weeks, we spent some time with the pups each day: picking each one up, petting it, and talking to it. We wanted our pups to be used to being handled. We also introduced them to sudden noises by thumping on the whelping box at times.

We started taking our puppies to work when they were one week old. As with all our litters, we have a whelping box in our office and our employees are encouraged to visit and handle the pups during their breaks. At night, Blanche and I each have a pup on our laps while we watch TV or read.

Puppies begin to stand at fourteen days, start to see at around sixteen days, walk at twenty-one days, and are sight and sound oriented at twenty-five days. Now the fun begins; your puppy will notice you and begin to walk and play. Our whelping box is located in our utility room and has a removable front door. When the pups are able to walk, we remove the door and let them crawl over the top. Once they are out, they are able to play in the utility room. When they climb out of the whelping box, we blow a whistle and call them, using the command *come*. Soon the pups associate the whistle and the *come* command, and scramble for the door to climb out. Often, one of the pups will hesitate to climb out and start to whine. We ignore its pleas. The pup sees its siblings out playing and soon gets up the courage to climb out on its own.

We want our pups to be bold, to explore and to learn on their own. It is best to resist the urge to help your young pup unless it is in trouble. When it's time to put them back in the box, we pick them up, place them in the box, and use the word *kennel*. The *kennel* command is very important, one the dog will hear throughout his life as he enters his crate, the car or truck, his bed, and every time you want to put him in a specific place.

At four weeks of age, the pups are fully weaned and are too big and rambunctious to leave in the whelping box, so we move them outside to our Scott

All of our pups get couch time.

elevated kennel system. I have a small carpet-covered ramp that I built for the pups to learn to climb into their kennel. Here again, I use the *kennel* command. This early training of the *kennel* command also helps in teaching the dog to load up when you take him hunting or to the vet. Since I have a pickup truck with a dog box and dog compartments on top, I want my dogs to climb the ramp and get into the truck on their own. Believe me, it's a lot easier to have them climb up on their own than for me to have to lift them up a half-dozen times every hunting trip.

At this point, we start feeding the pups in the outside kennel twice a day: in the morning and at night, right after a play session. I carry the food to the kennel, blow my whistle, and command the pups to *come*. I show them the food and then place it in the kennel. The pups soon learn to climb the ramp to get to their food. While they are climbing the ramp, I give them the *kennel* command. I also introduce the gun at this time. While the pups are chowing down on their meal, which is always a highlight for them, I stand away from them and fire my training pistol in the air. The training pistol makes only a light noise, but it aids in getting the pups used to loud sounds, and can help us identify any pup that might have sensitivity to loud noises or guns.

When letting the pups out for their playtime, I blow my whistle, open the kennel door, and command them to *come*. In a short period of time, the pups learn to come on the whistle and/or the *come* command, and they also know the *kennel* command. The best thing about this method is that the pups don't even know that they're being trained. They are simply responding to a favorable stimulus and to something they find enjoyable.

It's very important to continue bonding with your puppy. We sit on the ground with our pups for several minutes each day. The pups love to climb up on us, lick our faces, and be petted. We also carry small dog biscuits as special treats. Every time we call a puppy to us or have them kennel, we praise them and give them a treat.

Our house sits on eight acres of land. We do not have a manicured lawn; keeping, instead, the native short prairie grass, the same type of cover the pups will be hunting when they're older. This is their play area. Every day they explore and chase each other through the grass and brush.

The pointing instinct is inherent in puppies. At about six weeks or so, the pups start to point each other. One pup will stop and point, and the other pups will point back. Often, they will remain on point for several minutes. While being absorbed in play, they are teaching themselves staunchness on pointing and backing. When the pups start pointing each other, we introduce them to a pheasant wing tied to a fishing line. We've all done this at one time or another, and it's a fun little game for pups and handlers alike. At first the pups will try to pounce on the wing and chase it, but it's very important that they not be allowed to catch it. Soon they'll be pointing it; showing us the pointing instinct that's been bred for generations into them. While this is a fun game for all, and great for picture taking, we don't want to overdo it, thereby encouraging sight pointing. It's the nose that counts later on. Most importantly, we want the pups' first contact with feathers to be a great experience. At this point, we are simply bringing out their natural instincts, and we don't want anything bad to

Mom & pups go to the office with us.

happen to them. On the contrary, we want every experience to be positive and confidence building.

We made a lot of progress in the first six weeks, and most importantly, we had fun. There was no stress, no negative vibes. We now have pups that are well on their way to becoming great bird dogs. They love people, are intelligent, and are developing their talents to point, retrieve, and explore the cover.

Most owners pick up their puppies at seven to eight weeks of age, so some of this early training should have already been done. When you are looking for a breeder, keep this in mind when you ask them how they socialize their pups. Many professional breeders may not have the time to put in all the effort and attention that we do to our pups. However, they should be spending time with each litter to make sure that all pups have had plenty of time with humans in order to progress with their socialization. You can continue with this fun training as soon as you bring your pup home.

Pup pointing a wing, two pups backing the first.

Well socialized puppies love kids.

Puppy Training and Socialization:
Eight to Sixteen Weeks

At seven weeks of age, your pups are ready to be introduced to water, guns, and birds during play sessions in the field. In learning through play, each session is set up so that the pups will be in a positive and winning situation. During the next nine weeks, the pups are taken afield at least once a week. Each week we take the pups for about a half an hour run to areas with different features: woods, prairie with knee-high grass, streams, etc. We take all the pups along with the older dogs. At first the pups will chase the older dogs, but soon they venture into the woods and fields on their own, becoming bolder and more adventurous each week.

During these first field excursions, the pups are introduced to water. I choose a small stream for this, one that is about knee deep, has a slow moving current, and is about twenty feet wide. I prefer using streams to teach young puppies to swim instead of ponds. In a pond, you have to wade out and encourage the pup to swim out to you. In this situation the pup is always going into ever-deeper water, which can be very intimidating. We wade across the stream with the older dogs, calling and encouraging the pups to follow us. The pups can see the other side of the stream and can usually walk up to the bank once they have gotten through the deep part of the stream. If a pup hesitates, we continuing calling in a friendly manner, and start to walk away from the stream. Eventually, its desire to join us overcomes its fear and it crosses the stream.

In each of the following weekly outings, we cross a stream, staying with small streams at first and gradually working up to bigger water that is deeper and has a stronger current. After several weeks, the pups are used to water, sometimes crossing the stream ahead of us and waiting for us to join them.

When we have a new litter of puppies, we keep a covey of quail in a callback pen behind our house. Check the chapter on quail pens for a detailed diagram on how to build one. When using a callback pen, be sure to let one or two quail out at a time, making sure that there are several quail left in the pen, including a male. The quail left in the pen start whistling and call the quail back that you have released. At the bottom of the pen there is a small, funnel-shaped opening that the quail use to get back into the pen. This allows you to reuse the birds in your training sessions.

At six to seven weeks, the pups are introduced to birds by planting a quail in the tall grass behind our house. After covering the quail with grass so the puppy can't see it, we let one pup out, put it on a short lead, and start walking to the field. Then, releasing the pup from the lead, we tell the pup, *All right, hunt 'em up*. You can use any command you want; however, make sure that you use the same command every time you release your puppy into the hunting field. Soon the pup learns to associate this command with a hunting experience. With the puppy roaming out in front of us,

Pups learn at an early age to go up the ramp.

we give him plenty of time to find the planted bird. If he has a problem, we call the pup over to where the bird is planted.

A puppy can have a number of different reactions when it firsts smells a bird. Some will point the bird the first time; others may flash point and then attempt to grab the bird. One of our pups pointed the quail and then sat down. If your pup attempts to grab the bird, take hold of its lead and softly tell the pup, *Whoa*. Do not be hard on the pup because this introduction to birds should be fun. Every time the pup finds and points a bird, praise it, once again setting up a winning situation. After we have planted quail for our pups for several weeks, they know what is happening when we pass their kennel on the way to the quail pen. All the pups get very excited, and when I let the first pup out, it starts to search for the bird immediately. All of the puppies are usually pointing after several weeks.

After a pup holds point for a minute, Blanche flushes the quail. Standing about thirty feet away, I fire the blank gun when the quail flies. The pup has already heard a blank during feeding time. Now he starts to associate the sound of a gun with birds. The pup gets so excited that he doesn't even notice the gun. The quail usually flies thirty to fifty yards and then lands in thick grass. Quite often, the pup will start to chase the quail. I do not restrain him in the beginning; getting the pups supercharged on finding birds is the main objective. Many times, the pup will run ten yards or so and then stop to watch the quail land, then go over and hunt that area. In most cases, the pup will relocate the quail and point it, thus learning how to relocate singles. After the pup finds and points the quail a second time, I praise him, put a lead on, and take him back to the kennel. Taking another pup out, I let it hunt the same quail.

When all the pups are finding and pointing birds, I start letting two pups out at a time. We want to set up a situation in which the pups will learn to back. An older dog can be used for this, or you and a friend can train your pups together. When one of our pups finds and points a bird, the tendency for the other pup is to back and point the locating pup. When this occurs, we praise them both lavishly. I believe that backing is a genetic trait, inherent in dogs that come from good hunting stock. During play sessions in the field behind the house, our pups will often point each other. Sometimes, we have three or four pups all pointing and backing each other. I timed them several times and found that they would often stay pointing each other for three minutes or more.

We take the pups afield twice a week and have a pointing session with planted birds. As the weeks progress, the pups gain confidence and look forward to these sessions. What is especially gratifying is that the pups regard these sessions as playtime. In reality, they are learning to search the field, locate, and point birds, all while becoming accomplished swimmers. They are also getting used to gunfire and are associating it with birds. This is accomplished in non-stressful sessions in which the puppies have fun and always win. Praise and encouragement are used, rather than negative feedback. Following this method, at sixteen weeks old, the puppies are eager, confidant, and ready for their first wild bird hunt on opening day. I prefer to let my puppies work wild birds instead of planted birds. As soon as hunting season starts, I quit using planted birds and work our pup or puppies only on wild birds.

Opening day for grouse and Hungarian partridge is September 1 in Montana. Loading up the three remaining pups we kept from Annie's litter, as well as Annie and Duke, we headed to a ranch where we knew there were birds. Annie and Duke started covering the field with the pups following them. Coming over the top of a hill, we spotted Annie on point at the bottom of a coulee. All three pups were backing her! As we hurried excitedly down the hill, the pups held their points and as we reached the bottom, a covey of Huns exploded out of the brush. I knocked one down with my second shot, and Annie retrieved it. The rest of the covey spread out and flew over the hill. We climbed the hill, and the dogs started hunting the singles. Hershey, one of the pups, pointed right in front of me and when I moved in, a single flushed and I brought it down. Hershey charged over, picked it up, and brought it back to me. What a thrill it was to have a young pup point and retrieve its first bird!

Pups get regular field outings.

Basic Obedience and Good Canine Citizenship

Come, Out, Kennel, No, Sit, and Stay: These are some basic commands that you will want to teach your new puppy. These commands are essential to having a well-mannered dog in your house.

The *come* command is easily taught. Start calling your dog to you when you put his food down. Your pup will come running because he is hungry. When you get a play toy out or a dummy to teach him how to fetch, call, *Come.* Your pup will come running; he is excited and wants to play. Every time your dog readily comes, praise him. When he does not come when he is called, go get him, grab his collar, and lead him to where you want him to come, repeating the command.

Out is an essential command. You do not want your dog to mess up in the house. Make sure that you take your pup out every two or three hours. Every time you open the door, call him with the *come* command and, when he gets to the door, say, *Out.* Walk out with your dog and in a soft voice say, *Take care of yourself* or any other command you want to use. When your dog does his business say, *Good dog.* Dogs learn by association and repetition. Soon your dog will come to the door when you say *out.* I have a six-foot high chain-link fenced area in my yard that connects to our house, so I can let our dogs out to take care of themselves or to play. They soon learn to come at a run when I say *Out.*

Kennel means "go in". Every time you open the door to let your dog back in the house, use the *kennel* command. Every time you put your dog in his box or kennel run say, *Kennel*. When you put your dog up into your rig to go hunting use this command. I give my dogs a milk bone when I put them in their kennel for the night. They eagerly go into their boxes when they hear the *kennel* command. They know they are going to get a treat.

No is the first and most frequent command you will use on a young puppy. *No* means stop doing what you are doing: tearing up shoes, barking, messing up in the house, etc. Your dog will soon learn that your raised voice and *No* mean business.

Sit and *Stay*. Since I use my dogs for waterfowl hunting I use the *sit* and *stay* command. I want them to sit quietly by the blind or in the boat when we are hunting. Take hold of your dog's collar and push down on his rear end while you give the command, *Sit*. When your dog's butt hits the floor, praise him. In the beginning he will only sit for a few seconds. You can extend his sit by keeping your hand on his back and using slight pressure to keep his butt down. When you do this, praise him. When you give your dog a treat, give him the *sit* command. Do not give him the treat until he sits. He will soon sit because he wants his treat. One of the best treats for a dog is an ice cube. They love ice; it is a great treat, and it does not put weight on a dog. When we open the freezer to get ice our dogs come running. If you think your dog can't hear well, try this: When our dogs are in the bedroom far away from the kitchen and sound asleep, we try to open the freezer as quietly as possible. The dogs always hear it open and come running.

After your dog has learned to sit on command, you can teach the *stay* command. Step back and hold your hand up like a traffic cop. Use the command, *Stay*. If your dog moves before you release him, give him the *sit* command and make him sit again. Extend the time you make your dog stay until he understands that he is to stay where you put him until you release him. As always, make sure that you praise him every time he obeys.

The Proper Introduction of Your Puppy to Birds and the Gun

I really enjoy the many phone calls I receive from the readers of *Pointing Dog Journal*. I like helping folks with their training problems and it's great to hear all of the stories about how well their dogs are doing: the super bird hunt, the staunch point, the fantastic retrieve. However, I get three or four calls a year from dog owners describing the sad situation in which a dog is either gun-sensitive or gun-shy. Here is a typical scenario:

> *"My young pup has been doing a great job finding and pointing quail in the training field. Opening day of pheasant season, I invited my three hunting buddies to hunt with me. I was really excited to show off my new dog. Sure enough my pup found and pointed a cock pheasant in the first field. We all rushed up behind her and when the bird flushed we all got a shot at the bird. We were a little rusty in our shooting since we hadn't shot much since last year. It took a number of shots, but we finally killed the bird. After the bird fell I looked around and couldn't see my dog. I thought she had gone on ahead to find another bird. One of my buddies spotted her heading back to the rig. I called her but she refused to come. She crawled under the rig and no amount*

of coaxing could get her to come out. We finished our hunt without a dog. The next weekend my pup was eager to get into the rig. Then she saw me load my shotgun into the truck and she jumped out and ran back into the house. I guess I have a problem. What do I do now?"

The same scenario happens with a young puppy in the duck blind. Here the dog is confined in a blind, he is being restrained, he can't see the ducks, and all of a sudden two or three hunters stand up and start blasting away. By the end of the morning's hunt the dog is often scared to death at the sound of the gun. Gun-sensitive or gun-shy dogs are usually man made. However, some pups may have very soft and sensitive personalities that will require more time to be introduced to the gun. Unfortunately, a dog that is improperly introduced to the gun can quickly become gun-shy. Any trainer will tell you that curing a dog of being gun-shy is very difficult and time consuming. Many times it is an impossible task.

A dog's sense of hearing is far better than ours. Many trainers use silent whistles to train their dogs. A human cannot hear the whistle, but a dog can. Imagine how much better and more sensitive a dog's hearing is as compared to ours. That same heightened hearing makes a dog much more sensitive to loud sounds, especially the sound of a gun. I wear hearing protectors when I hunt. Even with hearing protectors, my ears are still sensitive to the sound of a shotgun. Believe me, if you and your hunting buddies shot two or three times each over my head in a matter of two or three seconds, I'd be heading back to the truck too!

In *"Dogs: A Startling New Understanding of Canine Origin, Behavior and Evolution"* the authors, Raymond and Lorna Coppinger, talk about the fact that very young puppies up to sixteen weeks of age have little or no fear. These early weeks are an ideal time to introduce your puppy to the gun.

Hopefully your breeder has started with loud noises when the puppies were still in the whelping box with their mother. With our litters, we rap the side of the box with our hands when the pups are every young. When they are old enough to start eating dog food, usually at three to four weeks, and are eagerly waiting for us to feed them, we bang the dog food bowls a few times. You can continue this by getting your pup used to loud sounds when he is doing something he really enjoys. You will find that he does not even pay attention to the noise.

Introducing your pup to the sound of a gun is a very important step in his training. I use a method for doing this that results in the dog having a positive association with the sound of the gun. You want him to get excited when he sees the gun. You want your puppy to associate the sound of the gun to the things he loves most: eating, playing, and finding and chasing game birds. Make the introduction in gradual steps, building up from a cap or blank gun with crimps to the sound of a shotgun. When you pick your puppy up and take him home, spend the first few weeks socializing him to you and your family and his new surroundings. When he is comfortable and accepts his new home, start your gradual process of introducing him to the sound of the gun. I take this in gradual steps, carefully observing how the pup reacts to each new noise.

If you feed your puppy outside, fire a blank gun one time when your dog is chowing down. Do this at least fifty feet away from the dog. Your dog will soon associate the sound of the gun with eating, which is a pleasurable experience for him. Watch for any reaction to the sound of the gun. In most cases your puppy will not even pay attention to the sound; he will be too busy eating.

Young puppies love to play and run. I recommend that you take your young dog out into the field at least twice a week. They need the exercise and you want them to start learning to explore and search. An ideal situation is to run your puppy with another dog. The puppy will be interested in running after and playing with the other dog. When your dog is out in front of you at least twenty yards and having fun, fire your blank gun one time. Your dog will probably not even notice the sound; he is out in the field having a great time. The sound of the gun is just a mild noise in the background. Gradually increase the number of times you fire the gun to two or three times a session. Be careful not to fire the gun in quick succession, but wait two or three minutes between firings. Take your shotgun with you on these outings. Let your puppy see you load your gun into your rig. You want your puppy to associate his going into the field with the sight of a shotgun.

If a young dog is properly introduced to guns, he will learn to love the sight and sound of the gun. My dogs get excited every time I get my shotgun out. They crowd by the door waiting to get into the truck to go hunting. My dogs have a positive association with the gun. Their greatest desire in life is to hunt birds. They know that the gun is part of the hunt, and that means they are going to get a chance to do what they love most. Dogs read their owners well. A young puppy will soon associate loading the shotgun in the rig with the fact that he is going to be taken for a run. Soon the pup will start to get excited when he sees me with my shotgun. This is the positive association I want him to make. I want him to know that when he sees a gun it means he is going out into the field to have a great time. Now, when I run my puppy, I will carry the shotgun over my shoulder. I am still firing the blank gun. However, I want my pup to get used to seeing me with my shotgun. When I start firing the shotgun with blanks it will be an easier transition for the puppy because he already has a positive feeling towards the shotgun.

I recommend that you introduce your young puppy to birds at an early age. There are many public game lands in most states that allow bird dog training. Almost all of the hunting clubs or bird dog clubs have access to land for training. Pigeons, quail, and chukars are the best birds to use when you start training a young dog.

Plant a quail in the field, and then let your puppy roam out in search of the bird. At first he will be curious and will be a little anxious because the bird is new to him. It only takes one or two sessions before your puppy will start pointing the bird. When you know that your pup is really excited about the bird, start using the blank gun again. You do not want to use the gun when the puppy first encounters a bird. Remember, the gun must be introduced as a positive association to the puppy. Young puppies will flash point and then flush and chase the bird. Wait until they are chasing the bird before you fire the gun. Each time the young puppy finds and chases a quail, move a little closer to him when you fire the blank gun. When the pup is totally turned on to birds and is at least eight to ten weeks of age, increase the sound by using a blank load in your shotgun. Often called a popper load, it is used in field trails and dog training. It is a shotgun shell with a light load of powder and no shot. The sound is about half as loud as the sound of a regular low brass shot shell. Another alternative to using blank loads is to use primer-loaded empty shells. Now you only have the light sound of the primer going off. The first time you use a blank load in the shotgun, stand at least seventy-five yards away from the dog. Over the next several weeks, move closer to the dog until you are able to fire the blank within twenty feet.

Always observe your dog. The puppy should be so excited about the bird that he pays absolutely no attention to the sound of the gun. If he shows any sign at all of nervousness or appears at all bothered by the sound, back off. Go back to the beginning. Get him into the bird and let him chase with no sound from you. Then start back with the cap gun or blank pistol. If you have followed the steps carefully, you should not have any problems. The key is that every time the dog hears the sound of the gun he is doing something he loves: eating, playing, hunting. He associates this sound in a positive way.

In the final stage, use a light loaded shotgun shell and repeat the process. Start seventy-five yards from the dog when he is working a bird, and only fire when the bird is flushed. Gradually move up to about twenty feet away from the dog. Never stand directly over a young dog when you fire a gun, but position yourself to the side of the dog. The sound of a gun over a dog's head can be deafening and frightening.

Even though your puppy has been successfully introduced to the gun and associates it with hunting, you still have to be careful not to expose him to too much noise. A young dog that is suddenly exposed to the sound of multiple shots in a matter of seconds can quickly become gun shy. One minute you have a bold puppy that pays no attention to the gun and the next minute you have a puppy that is blinking birds or heading back to the truck. During your dog's first hunting season, don't shoot directly over your dog's head; come into the dog's point of view from the side. If you are hunting with a friend, let him flush the bird while you shoot from the side, at least twenty feet away. Try to kill the bird with one shot. Never fire more than two shots at any one bird. That means two shots total: not two shots per hunter. Only one hunter should shoot at a time. You and your hunting partners should take turns shooting. One of you should be observing your dog to see how he handles the birds and if he has any reaction to the gun. If your hunting buddies don't understand the situation and want to blast away, I strongly suggest that you hunt your young dog alone during his first season. They probably won't be around to help you over the long months it will take to correct the problem of a gun-shy dog, or come up with the huge sum of money it will cost to pay a trainer to correct the problem. If you take the time to correctly introduce your puppy to the sound of the gun, doing it in gradual stages, and making it a part of the things your dog loves in life: food, play and hunting, you will have a dog that loves the sight and sound of the gun.

Here are some tips on what to avoid:

- Dogs are often afraid of fireworks, even adult dogs that have had years of hunting experience and love the sound of a gun. Fireworks have a much louder and much more shrill sound than a gun. Try to minimize your dog's exposure to this sound.
- Do not let anyone shoot smurf balls or bb guns at your dog. You want your dog to love the sight of a gun, not to be afraid of it.
- Do not take your dog to a gun club or shooting range to introduce him to the sound of a gun. Let's analyze the situation. You bring your young dog to a strange environment. He is apprehensive and nervous. The scene is strange to him and he is not having fun; he is restrained on a lead, and now he hears all of these loud sounds: bang, bang, bang, over and over again, hundreds of times. Where is the positive association? How is the dog having fun? Soon he will start to jump at loud sounds. Sure there is the occasional dog that can survive this scenario. However, many dogs will develop a negative association to the sound of the gun in this situation.

Six month old Chukar hunting with Duke.

The Importance of Reading Your Bird Dog

One of the best compliments that one dog man can give to another is to state, "He really knows how to read a bird dog". That means the man is able to observe a dog and tell by his body language and other mannerisms what the dog is doing and thinking. Learning how to read a bird dog is not an easy one- or two-step lesson; it is an evolving process that takes a lifetime. I have spent forty years with bird dogs and I continue to learn more about how and why and what a dog is doing with every new dog and with every passing year.

Dogs don't send us written letters and they don't talk to us in the English language. However, they communicate with us in other ways. A dog lets you know what he is doing through his body language. He talks with his eyes, his head, his tail, his nose, and the movement of his whole body. You need to observe your dog and concentrate on his body language in order to understand his actions.

Reading your dog is important for three reasons: monitoring your dog's health, improving your ability to train your dog, and being successful in the hunting field. Each dog is different and has different mannerisms. You have to learn the particular mannerisms of each one of your dogs in order to be successful in reading them. The basis of your relationship with your hunting dog is based on your bond with him.

This is the most important connection an owner can have with his dog. As you bond with your dog and a mutual trust builds between the two of you, you will have built the foundation for working with and reading your dog. Your dog will also learn very quickly how to read you. He knows by the sound of your voice and your body language, what your feelings are. Dogs learn how to read their owners far better than their owners learn how to read them.

Let's look at some examples of a dog's actions and how to read them. Last year, there were over seventy dogs that died of heat prostration on the opening day of pheasant season in one of the western states. I can guarantee you that all of those dogs gave definite signs to their owners that they were in physical trouble before they collapsed. Because their owners either could not read their dogs or were too busy shooting birds that they ignored the signs, their dogs died. Here are some of the signs a dog sends out when he becomes overheated. The first sign is the length of his tongue. A dog sweats and expels perspiration through his tongue. When he gets hot, his tongue hangs out of his mouth and is dripping with moisture. The dog will also start to pant or breath heavily; his chest will be going in and out on a rapid basis as he tries to get air to cool down. The dog will slow down his pace; he will often stop and lay down. Dogs will try to find a shady spot to get out of the sun. They will also try to dig a hole in the dirt. They are digging down in the dirt because it is cooler underneath the surface. Any one or all of these signs should alert you that your dog is experiencing physical problems and is in danger of heat exhaustion. You need to stop your hunt immediately, give your dog water and find a shady area, if possible, to rest him. This is just one example of the importance of reading a dog.

In order to be successful in training your dog, you have to be able to read his reactions to your training sessions with him. Is your dog accepting the training? Is he using avoidance tactics to avoid the training? Do you know when it is time to end the session? If you cannot read your dog during training, it is going to be very difficult for you to make progress and successfully train your dog.

The dog's intense point tells you he has the bird.

Let's say you are working with your dog on water retrieves. You throw a dummy and your dog goes to the water, stops, and starts drinking from the pond. Or your dog goes over to the side and starts eating grass. He might leave your side and start running the bank. These are all signs that the dog is avoiding going into the water. He might be afraid of the water or he might just be showing a stubborn streak. Let's look at training a dog to retrieve a dead bird in the field. You either shoot a bird or plant a dead bird in the field. You send your dog out for the retrieve, knowing exactly where the bird is located. Watch him closely. You can tell by his use of nose and his head position if he knows where the bird is laying. If he knows and runs by the bird, going off in another direction to search, then there is a good chance he is avoiding the retrieve. Dogs are smart; they will seldom flat-out refuse to do what you want. They will pretend they are trying to obey you by searching elsewhere when they actually know where the bird is.

However, a dog can also become confused and not know what you want him to do in a training session. He might communicate this to you by holding his tail down. His body might go into a crouch position and he might lower his head. Look at his eyes. If they look confused and nervous, chances are your dog doesn't understand what you want him to do. In this case, you need to get him to relax. Try to show him again in a clearer way what you want him to accomplish. Punishing him will only confuse him more and set back your training program. Looking at your dog's eyes is an excellent way of reading his actions and intentions. Dogs are honest. If they look you straight in the eye and hold eye contact, they are telling you, "OK, I want to work with you and do what you want me to do". If a dog turns his head to one side and refuses to look at you, then you probably are having a problem. In this case the dog is refusing to cooperate with you. By reading your dog, you can make much greater progress in your training sessions, eliminate or

Look where the dog's nose is pointing.

Dog is overheated and needs rest.

avoid problems, and end up with a much better trained dog.

Reading your dog during the actual hunt can make the difference between a great hunt, where the two of you work as a team and put birds in the bag, and a hunt where there are many missed opportunities because you and your dog were not in sync. Every dog works birds differently. Chukar, my male GWP, works his birds with a high head. He also points them from a great distance. If he locates birds close to him, his body will be intense and he will quiver with anticipation. He will point with his front end low to the ground and his rear end high in the air. I can tell by his pointing intensity and his body position just how close the birds are in front of him. One of my females, Hershey, almost always points with a flagging tail. The rest of her body is intense. She flags because of her excitement at finding birds. When I approach her, I have learned to give her a release command. I will say, "All right". If the birds are right in front of her, she will not move and her tail will go rigid. That's Hershey's way of telling me, "I've got them pinned right here in front of me! Go flush them and shoot them!" If the birds have moved out, she will relocate on the release and pin them again.

Observe where your dog's head is pointing. If your dog's head is pointing to the left and the wind is coming from that direction then the chances are great that the bird will be to the dog's left. I know this sounds elementary, but I have seen a number of hunters who don't follow the dog's nose and head direction when trying to locate the pointed bird. Watch your dog when you kick the brush to flush the bird. If the bird is right there, the dog will tense up and move back on his heels in anticipation of the flush. Trust your dog. If you can't find the bird and you release your dog to relocate and it stays on point refusing to move, chances are great that the bird is still there. Look again. Sometimes I have gotten down on my hands and knees and found a bird buried deep in the grass or the brush.

We expect a great deal of our dogs. And, our dogs have the right to expect us to understand the signals that they send us so we can work successfully with them as a team to produce birds. One of the keys to learning to read your dog is for the two of you to spend time together, especially out in the bird field. The more actual exposure you and your dog have working on wild birds, the better hunting team you will become.

Five-month-old wirehair retrieving sharptail.

Training Your Young Bird Dog:
A New Approach

For hundreds of years men have been working to selectively breed superior bird dogs. These efforts have been focused on improving the dog's inherited natural abilities: an outstanding nose that can smell the scent of a game bird, the strong desire to hunt, the ability to search the field, and the instinct to point. All of these qualities are essential to the make up of a good bird dog.

The training you do with your young pup should focus on bringing out and developing your pup's inherent natural abilities. Unfortunately most dog owners put most of their training emphasis on controlling their dogs. Go out to most bird dog clubs and you will see a line of men with their young dogs on check cords. They are waiting their turn to go out into the field where there is a planted bird. They restrain their pup as he approaches the bird, hoping to get a point. The bird is flushed and then the owner leads his pup away and the next owner comes into the field. Sound familiar? It's like putting the cart before the horse. Don't get me wrong, a finished bird dog should be whoa trained and should have an intense point. However, it is my belief that you put the controls on the dog after you have let him develop his natural abilities. My revolutionary training approach in this book is to divide your training into two parts. The first part takes place from the time you get your puppy at seven to ten weeks until he is at least one year old and has had one wild bird season.

There is little formal training during this stage. Sure you want to teach your pup to *come*, to *kennel* and also what *No* means. The most important aspect is to bond with your dog. You want your dog to believe that you are the most important person in the world. His life should revolve around you. You're the one who will introduce him to the gun, water, retrieving, and birds. You will be exposing him to wild birds in the field. This is the time to let him explore, to discover the big world, to find out how much fun it is to go hunting with his master, to ride in the car with him, or to be by his side at night. Let your dog enjoy his first year. Let him have fun. Don't worry about busted birds; he will soon learn to start pointing. Bonding with your dog, letting him have fun, exposing him to wild birds and hunting, and lavishing him with praise when he does things right, will give your young dog the opportunity to fully develop his natural instincts and talents to become an outstanding bird dog. Don't use the e-collar and don't try to keep your dog in close. Trust me, he won't get lost. After your dog is one year old and has developed his natural abilities, you will start the second part of your training. Here is where you put on the controls. Teach your dog whoa training, the trained retrieve, and honoring point.

Let's look at the seven hereditary characteristics that we want to develop in your puppy during the first part of his training. The North American Versatile Hunting Dog Association has a test for young dogs up to sixteen months of age. Other versatile dog organizations like the VDD have similar tests. NAVHDA's Natural Ability Test was started to measure seven hereditary characteristics of a bird dog that are essential to his make-up. These inherited abilities usually show up in a dog at an early age. You want to take advantage of this fact and spend your first year or two helping your dog develop these traits to his fullest. Here are eight inherited characteristics:

- **Nose**: The quality of a hunting dog's nose is the single most important attribute that a dog can possess. If your dog can't smell the birds, he can't find them. The better your dog's nose, the more birds he will be able to find. A dog's ability to smell is far greater than a human's. All dogs have the ability to smell, however the quality of a dog's nose varies from dog to dog. It is important to pick a pup from a breeder who has developed a line of dogs that have a good nose. While the quality of a dog's nose is inherited, you can help the dog learn to use his nose to its maximum effectiveness.

- **Search**: The ability of a dog to cover the field to produce game for the hunter is the purpose of a dog's search. Throughout the search, your dog should display strong desire, stamina, and intense interest in finding birds. Your dog should develop the ability to adapt his search to the terrain. You don't measure your dog's ability to search based on his distance from you. A dog searching a thick grouse cover will work close to the hunter. A dog covering the prairies will adjust his search to stretch out and cover the vast area in which he is hunting. A good search is the result of your dog covering the ground so that no game is missed

- **Pointing**: An intense stylish point is a thrilling sight. Your dog should have an intense point that is also productive. There is a huge difference between a dog with an intense point and a dog that merely stops and stands when he finds birds. The quality of a dog's point adds to the pleasure of the hunt.
- **Desire to work**: The strong never-ending desire to work is demonstrated in all aspects of the dog's performance. Desire shows itself in the dog's search, pointing, water work, cooperation, and retrieving.
- **Cooperation**: Your dog and you are a team. You both have a common goal: to produce game for the bag. Your dog needs to show that he is cooperating with you during all phases of his performance in both the field and the water. Cooperation should not be confused with a dog that is reined in and working just a few feet in front of the hunter. Over-control of your dog is not cooperation. Your dog can be out on the chukar slopes 500 yards in front of you and still be performing his job properly and cooperating fully with you. A cooperative dog is not over dependent on the handler. He is a self-assured dog that knows his job and performs it well while working as your hunting partner.
- **Waterwork**: We own versatile dogs because we want hunting dogs that are able to perform equally well on both upland birds and waterfowl. A dog for that purpose must have a love of the water, one that has the strong desire to go into the water to search for and retrieve waterfowl.
- **Tracking**: The ability of your dog to track wounded game is very important. Many times during the hunting season, you will knock a bird down that runs away. Your dog's ability to track and find the wounded bird will result in bringing far more game to the bag. As ethical hunters, it is important that we make every attempt to recover all wounded game. A bird dog that excels in tracking is extremely valuable to the hunter.
- **Retrieving**: While retrieving is not tested in the NAVHDA natural ability test, I am going to include it in our early training program. I believe that retrieving is an inherited natural instinct, especially in versatile gun dogs. It is an important part of the total package of a complete bird dog.

In future chapters we are going to analyze each of these eight characteristics and how you can help your hunting dog to develop them to their fullest extent. I urge all of my readers to contact NAVHDA and find out about your local chapter and the natural ability test. The natural ability test is a great way to judge your young dog's potential. It is also a lot of fun. You can contact NAVHDA on the web at www.navhda.org or call 1-847-253-6488.

A group of veratile dog owners training for NAVHDA test.

Camas
Bringing a New Pup Home

In July of 2005, Blanche and I picked up a new eight-week-old pup from Jeff Funke's Three Devils Kennel. Our new pup is a Verein Deutsch-Drahthaar female. Drahthaar is the word for wirehair in German. The VDD is a breed club for drahthaar's. Most people would regard these dogs as German wirehaired pointers. However, the VDD organization is very firm in stating that their dogs are drahthaar's. They have their own testing program, similar to the NAVHDA testing program but with a greater emphasis on tracking. They also have breed wardens who approve your dog for breeding.

We named our new pup Camas, after the western prairie flower of the same name. Camas was brought into our home and introduced to the rest of our pack: Belle and Hershey, ten-year-old German wirehairs who are sisters, and Chukar, our five-year-old German wirehair male. The first week was like hell week, with Camas learning the *No* word and establishing a relationship with the other dogs as well as beginning her bonding with us. We also started her training with basic commands: *Come, Kennel,* and the most important one for a young puppy, *No.*

At the end of the first week we took all of our dogs out to a section of state game land where we do our dog training and conditioning. There is a spring creek that runs through the middle of the section, so the dogs can jump in and cool off. The spring creek is about three to four feet deep and averages about twenty feet wide. It is a perfect stream to introduce a young dog to water. We let our dogs run for thirty minutes twice a week as part of their conditioning program. As soon as the older dogs were let out of the truck they took off. Camas ran after them and tried to keep up, but her short puppy legs wouldn't let her. When they disappeared she would come back to us, but every time the older dogs circled and came back to us, Camas would join them and try her best to keep up with them. Camas showed no fear of the high cover in the field. Whenever she was out in front of us at least twenty yards, I fired a blank from my training pistol. I would fire four or five times during each outing. Camas paid no attention to the sound of the gun. She was too excited about running with the other dogs.

The temperature during our runs was in the high 80s to low 90s. After a twenty-minute run, our three older dogs would jump into the spring creek to cool off. Camas was reluctant to get in the water. You could tell that she wanted to, but was a little timid about this new experience. I jumped into the creek, crossed it, and called all of the dogs to me. The older dogs followed me. Not wanting to be left behind, Camas soon jumped in the water and swam across the creek to me. I then re-crossed the creek and all of the dogs, including Camas, followed me. We let the dogs run for another ten minutes and then I repeated the creek crossing. This time, Camas was one of the first dogs to jump in; she didn't wait for the other dogs.

We ran all of our dogs two to three times a week for the rest of July and August. As Camas grew and her legs got longer she was able to keep up with the other dogs. Now she was ranging out from fifty to one hundred yards, searching the field and jumping in the creek on her own. She displayed a great deal of boldness and enthusiasm. These runs were a great introduction to the same type of cover Camas would be working during hunting season. I continued to fire the blank pistol on each outing. During the last two weeks in August, I started using popper shotgun loads. A popper load is a shotgun shell with no lead and about half the powder of a regular shell. It makes a louder sound than a blank gun but not as loud as a regular shot load. Camas did not pay any attention to the sound of the gun. After several outings, Camas would get excited when I would take my shotgun out of the gun cabinet at home. She knew that meant that we were going for a run and had associated the gun with something she really loved to do.

Socialization with Us and the Other Dogs

During the summer weeks, Camas would come to the office along with the other dogs. She learned to socialize with our staff and the people who come in to our office, such as the UPS and FedEx drivers, customers, and friends. Camas was also learning the pecking order with Belle, Hershey, and Chukar. She and Chukar soon bonded and they would play with each other for hours on end. Belle and Hershey tried to ignore her and pretend she didn't exist. When Camas invaded their territory or tried to take one of their dog bones, they quickly put her in her place. They would either growl at her or grab her by the neck and Camas would immediately flatten herself on the floor.

With four dogs, it is important that they all get along and establish their place in the pack. All four of our dogs are housedogs, and they all travel and hunt with us. If a dog cannot get along with the other dogs, then problems occur. While all four of our dogs spend time in the house, Chukar and Camas sleep outside in our Scott kennels. Camas has a very thick and dense coat and, like Chukar, has no problem sleeping outside. Either Blanche or I would have Camas on our lap for a short time every evening. We continued to spend time with her and develop a bond with her. At the same time we were teaching her to come and training her to go to the door when she had to go out to take care of herself.

Camas takes a swim with our older dogs.

Introduction to Retrieving

Camas was born with a desire to retrieve. The week we got her we threw a dead duck into a pond, Camas went into the water at swimming depth and retrieved the duck. Camas, like most puppies, liked to pick things up and carry them around: shoes, socks, Blanche's purse, etc. I started throwing a small dummy for Camas on our deck. The deck is fenced so she could not run away from me with the dummy. She loved to play this game. I then took her out to our fenced-in yard and put a long lead on her. I would throw the dummy and she would run out and pick it up. She wanted to play with it; she would throw it in the air and pick it up again. I would give the *fetch* command when I sent her for the dummy and then, when she had it in her mouth, I would say, *Fetch* and gently pull her toward me.

When I tried throwing the dummy for her without her being on a lead she would go out to pick it up and then play the try-and-catch-me game. Camas did not want to give up the dummy. At this stage when she was only twelve weeks old, I did not want to come down hard on her and dampen her enthusiasm. I continued to throw the dummy for her, but only when I had her on a long lead and could make her bring it back to me. She showed me a natural desire to retrieve. I will force break her after she has had a full year of bird hunting.

Eight-week-old Camas retrieves a duck.

First Introduction to Birds: Sixteen Weeks Old

Every August, I use pigeons in an automatic release trap to re-enforce steadiness with my older dogs. I put out two traps in a bird field with a pigeon in each trap. I try to hide the traps so the dogs cannot see them. We put all of the dogs on a stake and chain at the start of the bird field so they can watch and hear what is going on. I put an e-collar on the dog that will be going into the field. Blanche works the transmitter for the e-collar while I take my gun. When the dog makes bird contact and points, I have Blanche release the trap and I shoot the bird. If the dog moves before the shot or before I give it the command to fetch, Blanche hits the low intensity button on the e-collar. This gives the dog a buzzing sound and a very low stimulation for a brief second. That is enough to remind the dog to remain steady to wing, shot, and fall. All of my older dogs have been whoa trained using birds, automatic release traps, and the e-collar. They only need a short session to refresh their training before the hunting season begins. Both Belle and Hershey were totally steady for both of their birds. They did not need any reminder with the collar. Chukar moved after the shot on the first bird but the e-collar stopped him. He was totally steady on his second bird. Camas watched each of the dogs work their birds and she heard the shots and the praise when the dogs retrieved the birds.

After Belle, Hershey, and Chukar had their turn I planted two birds for Camas. I did not use the e-collar on her. I put her on a long check cord. I released her and let her run free. I did not hold the check cord. The purpose of the check cord was to bring her back to me after she picked up the dead bird. Camas tore out into the field and scented the first bird. She pointed and Blanche released the bird. Camas watched the bird fly and was steady to flush and shot. As soon as the bird started to fall she raced out and grabbed it. I followed so that I could grab the end of the check rope. This was one of the first times she had a bird in her mouth. She smelled it, licked it, and kept picking it up. When she had it in her mouth I gave the *fetch* command and pulled her to me. I praised her and let her hold the bird for a few moments. I wanted her to really enjoy the moment. I gently opened her mouth and took the bird from her while giving the command *give*, and then I quickly put the bird in my vest. Camas was already running the field, looking for another bird. When she smelled the second bird, she charged the trap. Blanche released the bird before she got to it. The pigeon catapulted into the air and then flew down into thick brush only five feet from the release trap. Camas could smell the bird but she could not see it, due to the heavy cover. She locked up on an intense point. I went in, flushed, and shot the bird for her. Camas went out and picked up the pigeon. I grabbed the check cord and gently pulled her to me, repeating the same sequence as the first bird.

Camas impressed me with her strong desire, her nose (she smelled both birds at about twenty yards), and her intense point on the second bird. With that much desire and ability, I decided that all of her future exposure and bird work would be on wild birds during hunting season. Too many things can go wrong using planted birds. The young dog can catch the bird, and they can smell you on the bird. They also soon learn that this is a game and, instead of doing a search, they quickly learn where you put the traps. In a real hunting situation your dog might have to hunt for an hour or more before it makes bird contact. A young dog has to learn to hunt hard and develop its search and desire. Wild birds are the best way to develop this in a young dog. Hunting season in Montana starts on September 1 for Huns, mountain grouse and sharptails. Camas' next exposure would be on wild birds in eastern Montana.

Camas points and holds while I flush a pigeon out of the trap.

First Wild Bird Hunt - Learning to Track:
Seventeen Weeks Old

Blanche and I have a small house in eastern Montana where we do most of our bird hunting. There is an abundance of upland birds and fairly good duck and goose hunting. There is also a great deal of Block Management in our area. Block Management is a program through which private ranches allow public hunting in return for payment by the state. It is an outstanding program that has opened several million acres to hunting.

September is often the hottest month of the year in Montana. We try to start our hunts early, and finish by 10:00am or 11:00am when the temperature normally reaches eighty degrees. I will not hunt my dogs when it gets that hot. We also carry water in our game vests and stop frequently to rest our dogs. Each dog gets about thirty to forty-five minutes of hunting time.

I usually like to hunt one dog at a time. However, during the beginning of the season, I let Camas hunt with one of the older dogs. Each day I let her hunt with a different dog. At first Camas would go out with the older dog for about fifty yards, and then come back to us and hunt close. After a few minutes she would range out again. She was learning to search and gaining confidence. The first day we shot two sharptail with Hershey. Camas was not hunting. When we got back to the truck, I watered Hershey and put her up. I took the sharptail, opened the door to Camas' box and let her smell the bird. I closed the door, tied a rope to the sharptail, pulled some feathers, and left them on the ground. I laid the sharptail on the ground in front of the feathers and then dragged the dead bird through the grass for about fifty yards. I made one turn of about thirty degrees in the drag. I got Camas out of her box, put a lead on her, and walked her to where the feathers were on the ground. I gave her a command to track and let go of the lead. She smelled the feathers and immediately started to follow the track. She followed it for about twenty yards and temporarily lost it. She backtracked, picked it up again, and this time smoked the track quickly, following it right to the bird. I let her pick the bird up and hold it, giving her lavish praise and telling her what a great dog she was, while I gently stroked her side. You could see the pride and enthusiasm in her gait and face.

Camas' First Track on a Wild Pheasant: Seventeen Weeks Old

In September after our morning hunts, we drive the back roads in the area to scout for new areas to hunt both upland birds and waterfowl. The day after Camas tracked the sharptail, we had a pheasant run across the dirt road we were on and go into a section of state land. This section was composed of high grass and thick cover with a brush row of trees along one edge. I stopped the rig and we watched the pheasant run through the field. I then got Camas out, put a lead on her, and led her over to where the pheasant had crossed the road. Blanche grabbed her camera and followed us. Camas scented the pheasant when she was about twenty yards from where it went into the cover. I released her and she immediately started to track it. She quickly followed the track for over a hundred yards. The pheasant went over to the brush row and crossed it into another field. When Camas was about ten yards from the brush row, I saw the pheasant take off from the other field. Camas tracked the bird through the brush row and right to where the bird flew. She impressed me with her excellent tracking ability and her use of nose.

Camas works a pheasant track.

First Contact with Sharptail: Eighteen Weeks Old

Early one September morning, we were driving to a large CRP area to hunt. Blanche spotted a group of six young sharptail grouse feeding in a wheat stubble field. We had permission to hunt this area, so I pulled off the road. The birds saw us and ran into the brushy fencerow. I knew that this was a great opportunity to get my young pup into birds that were still naïve about the hunting season. I got Camas out and the two of us starting walking up the fencerow.

Three sharptail flew out of the cover ahead of us. Camas did not have a chance to point them, however, she did see them fly. She sat down and watched them fly as I shot one. As soon as the bird hit the ground, Camas took off. She raced to the bird, picked it up and galloped back to me with the bird in her mouth. She stopped short and it took me several minutes of coaxing to get her to bring the bird to me. She was quite proud of herself. I let her hold on to the bird while I patted her side and praised her. I then gave her the release command and gently took the bird from her. I put the bird in my vest and we started walking up the fencerow again. I knew that all the young birds we saw feeding had not flushed with my first shot. One young sharptail flew out of the cover ahead of me. I shot the bird and Camas again raced out and brought the bird back to me. It was a great first wild bird experience for her. She was focused on the flying bird and paid no attention to the sound of the shot.

Camas watches as I shoot a sharptail.

Camas gallops back with the sharptail.

Camas' First Pheasant Hunt:
Twenty-One Weeks Old

The first week of pheasant season, I took Camas to a section of CRP where I had found a lot of pheasants the year before. Unfortunately, the cover was much thinner than last year and it appeared that the pheasants would not hold as well in the thin cover. As soon as Camas got into the field she got birdy. She moved into the field about twenty yards and went on point. I stepped in front of her and flushed a hen and Camas took off after the bird. I called her back but, before she got back to me, she got birdy again. She took off away from us, and Blanche and I watched her charge through the field and up a small hill. At the crest of the hill we saw birds explode into the air. There where at least fifteen pheasants in the air. Camas was really charged. She kept running around the top of the hill putting more birds in the air. I gave up trying to call her, and Blanche and I stood and watched.

Camas worked her way down the hill toward us, putting up two more pheasants. When she finally got to us, I stopped her, patted her, and let her calm down; keeping her by my side for at least five minutes. When she regained her breath and stopped panting, I let her go. She moved out in front of us and snapped on point. I took one step and another hen pheasant got up. We worked our way back to the rig and I gave Camas some water and put her up.

Most people would have considered this situation a disaster. Camas was running out of control and flushing birds way out of gunshot range. But I looked at this as a good experience for her. She showed me that she had great desire and she overcame any reluctance she had in the bird field. Now all tentativeness that she had about getting out and searching was gone. She became a very bold pup with an intense desire to find birds. I had faith that she would quickly learn how to handle birds and work them slowly and point them. She already had a strong pointing instinct. Camas was just overwhelmed with the large number of birds in one field.

Second Pheasant Hunt:
Twenty-One Weeks Old

The next day, Camas and I hunted another CRP field. This field had thick cover and, in past years, I had shot both sharptail and pheasant there. A wheat field bordered the CRP field, so the birds had both feed and cover in the same area. We hunted the field fairly early in the morning, about 9:00am. Camas went out and searched the field about forty yards in front of us. She quartered the field and hunted hard. At just over five months of age, she already was all business; no pottering around, no screwing with butterflies or mice, she was looking for gamebirds. Her instincts and the genetic hunting qualities she inherited from her parents and grandparents had kicked in. Camas had already figured out the program. It was a thrill to watch her work the field and sort out the bird scent.

After a half hour, we were hunting the edge of the field next to the wheat field when Camas slammed on point. Immediately, two cock pheasants sprang into the air. I fired my gun and one pheasant collapsed fifteen yards in front of me. Camas ran to where the bird fell and then took off, turning to the left and then running through the field and over the hill. I called her back, convinced that the bird was dead and lying right where it fell. I thought Camas was chasing the other pheasant that had flown away. I should have remembered that Camas had already tracked a pheasant for over one hundred yards just four weeks ago. I should have trusted her. After I spent five minutes looking for the downed pheasant with no luck, I went up over the hill where I last saw Camas. She was sitting on the other side of the hill, holding a live, wounded pheasant. She had tracked it over two hundred yards. She let me take the bird from her while I told her in a soft voice what a great dog she was. She wagged her tail and I could tell she was proud of herself. Next time I knew I could trust her. It is hard to go wrong, trusting a good bird dog. We often make the mistake of believing that we know more about game birds then our dogs do. They have much better noses than we have and a much better ability to find birds than we could ever hope to have.

Third Pheasant Hunt:
Twenty-Three Weeks Old

Blanche and I traveled back to eastern Montana for the third week of pheasant season. We hunted Camas on a ranch that had a small pond surrounded by cattails, in the middle of a section of CRP. Camas worked the area around the pond without getting birdy. When she came to a small depression that led up to the CRP field, she picked up her pace. I could tell by the way she used her nose and worked the area that she was birdy. Her whole body showed excitement. She carefully worked up the draw and pointed once, then moved on to the end of the draw and locked on point where the draw ended at a barbed wire fence. When she locked on point, I kicked the cover in front of her nose. Two cock birds exploded from the cover. One flew to my left; I shot, and saw the bird fall as I swung on the other cock bird that flew to my right. My shot hit the bird in the head and it fell to the ground. Camas ran to the second bird and picked it up and held it in her mouth. When I got to her I praised her and let her hold the bird for several minutes. Then I took it from her and we went over to where I saw the first bird fall. Camas tracked it for about thirty yards but then lost it. I brought in Chukar and Belle to help find the bird, but the older dogs lost the track at the same place as Camas. My guess is that the bird was not hit hard and flew away while I was picking up the other bird. In just a matter of days, Camas had made great progress in her hunting ability in searching for and finding pheasants. She already had established a very intense point and was using her nose.

At the end of October an old friend of mine, Bill Maxwell from Texas, came up to hunt with me. We took all four of my dogs with us to eastern Montana. Camas was now almost six months old. She had already spent over 20 days hunting wild birds. The first morning we hunted a section of rolling state land that held both sharptail grouse and pheasants. It wasn't long before we spotted two sharptail run from the wheat stubble field into the CRP. I stopped our rig about one hundred yards from where we saw the birds and put Camas down. She quickly got birdy and went on point. I took one step and a sharptail got up about twenty yards in front of us. Both Bill and I shot and missed. The sound of our guns flushed a group of about twenty sharptail another thirty-five yards in front of us; too far to shoot. This far into the hunting season, the sharptail were becoming very wary. We should have waited and not shot at the first bird. Camas ran up to where the group of sharptail got up and circled around, excited with the smell of fresh bird scent. We hunted her for another twenty minutes without any more bird contact.

Later that afternoon we hunted a series of small draws with Camas. At the beginning of the first draw Camas got birdy and started tracking. Every dog works birds differently. When you learn to read your dog, you will begin to learn the individual signs he gives off, letting you know he is on to birds. Camas works her birds with a low head and becomes very intense and deliberate. I like her slow, deliberate work because I can easily keep up with her. Camas tracked the birds for about fifty yards and then slammed on point. She stopped to point so suddenly that she had her left back paw in the air. I looked down and saw a cock and a hen pheasant in the grass in front of her. I flushed the birds and Bill killed the cock bird. Camas was steady at the flush; she stood and watched the birds fly and only broke after the shot. I had not done any training on steadiness with her yet. The steadiness she exhibited on this hunt she had inherited from her ancestors. By getting her out into the field, hunting wild birds and giving her the freedom to run and learn how to find and handle game birds, Camas was developing the natural ability that she was born with. Remember, I stated that 80% or more of a bird dog's ability comes from its genetic background. The key is to bring it out by exposing the dog to wild bird hunting.

The rest of the afternoon Camas worked and pointed five more pheasants. She held steady to flush and shot on the two cock birds that she had pointed. Camas is now very sure of herself. She loves hunting. When it is another dog's turn to hunt, she barks in her dog box. The third day of our hunt, I hunted Camas second. We hunted her for about an hour and then I called her to me. She refused to come. She knew I was going to put her up and hunt another dog and she did not want to quit. She was beginning to catch on to the game, and wanted to take control. While I had the e-collar on her for the last four weeks when she hunted, I had not used it. I put the collar on her to get her used to it and to associate it with the pleasure of hunting. I would put the collar on her just before I let her out of the box to hunt. She would hold still while I put it on her. She knew that when the collar was on, she got to hunt. If I got the collar out while she was on the ground she would run to me to have it put on. It took me about fifteen minutes to catch her and put her up. The next day at the end of her hunt, she again refused to come when called. This time I called her and gave her a shock. I kept the shock on until she started to come to me. As soon as she started to come, I stopped the shock and praised her. I only used number two on the shock collar, which is a medium level of shock. I hunted her later that day and had to use the shock one more time to get her to come. Those two lessons were all it took. For the rest of the week, she came quickly when called, and I did not have to use the shock collar for the rest of the season.

Sharptail

Bill and I hunted a coulee filled with brush. At the mouth of the coulee, Camas went on point. Bill and I walked in and flushed a large covey of sharptail. The group split up and half flew to the north and the other half flew to the south. I knocked down one bird; I saw it fall and then get up and run up the side of the coulee. Camas was looking the other way at the other group of sharptail. I called her to me and took her up to where I saw my bird fall and gave her a command to track. She put her nose down and followed the bird over the hill and down a barbed wire fence. After fifty yards the fence made a ninety-degree turn to the right. Camas continued to track the bird down the fencerow. After another fifty yards she jumped through the fence and grabbed the wounded sharptail. I was impressed at how well and how fast she was able to track the bird.

Locked up on a sharptail.

Thanksgiving Hunt

Blanche and I went back to eastern Montana for what turned out to be our last upland bird hunt of the year. The Sunday after Thanksgiving, a huge snowstorm hit the area and ended our hunt. During this last hunt, Camas showed the confidence and hunting ability of a dog much older than her seven months. On every outing she found and pointed both sharptail grouse and pheasant. She held her point and allowed me to flush and shoot before she broke. Camas would run out and pick up the bird and hold it and bring it back to me. She possesses a very strong prey drive and wants to keep the bird. I am not worried about that. I will force break her to retrieve this coming spring. The first hunting season I wanted to build up her prey desire. Retrieving, like whoa training, is part of the second season when you start to put the controls on your dog after he has had one year of wild bird hunting to develop all of his natural abilities. Camas had shown us that she possessed very strong natural abilities, and her great desire would help her in getting through the lessons she would learn before her next hunting season.

Retrieving pheasant.

Camas:
Range-Search-Cooperation

During one of Camas' first hunting experiences, I put her in the field with one of our older dogs. Camas tried heartily to keep up with the older dog. Each field trip, as she gained confidence and grew bigger and had the physical ability to run better, she continued to expand her range. In the beginning she would only go out fifteen to twenty-five yards and then she would come back to me. After several weeks I ran her by herself. Now she started to expand her range. Camas improved her range and hunting ability each time she was put into the hunting field. Every time she made bird contact, she built up her desire. I watched her learn how to handle the birds. In the beginning she pushed her birds. After a few bird contacts, she started to use caution and worked the birds slowly. The result showed in her pinning and pointing pheasants and sharptail grouse.

I kept my commands to a bare minimum during this time. When I wanted to change her direction, I would use the *come around* command with my voice and turn in the direction that I wanted her to go. She soon figured out what I wanted. She also began to start looking back and checking on me. I like my dogs to stay out in front, but to maintain contact by checking with me. They do this by coming back to a distance of about twenty-five yards away from me and looking at me. If I do not call them to me when they check with me, they know they should continue hunting.

Camas showed great progress in her hunting ability in every hunt. I could watch her and see the improvement in the way she covered the field, hunted objectives, and worked the birds. She was gaining bird smarts. Sometimes the birds would outfox her and she would lose them. However, each bird contact was a great learning experience for her.

Camas got the opportunity to hunt wild birds for forty days in this, her first season. I tried to hunt her in areas that I knew from past hunts had an abundance of birds. I also varied the terrain. Camas hunted CRP fields, willow groves, and coulees. She learned that every area has hot spots for birds. Soon she figured out the different objectives and areas that were likely to contain birds. What amazed me was her moxie in not pushing her birds. She had an intense point and was careful not to push the birds into flushing. She also held point and let me flush the bird. During the last few weeks of the season, Camas stayed steady through flush and shot. She would watch the bird fly away and would normally not break until she saw it fall. Then she would run out and grab it.

The opportunity that Camas had to hunt wild birds enabled her to develop her natural ability. She wasn't held back or distracted by my trying to micro manage her and she wasn't confused by too many commands. If you try to put controls on your young dog too soon and if you keep yelling at him, trying to control his search, he will become totally dependent on you and will never learn how to search and find birds. A micro-managed dog will also quickly loose his desire to hunt. He will always be afraid of making a mistake and getting punished for it.

The only time I used any force on Camas was at twenty-three weeks, when she would not come to me. It only took two short lessons with the e-collar to get her to understand what I expected of her. After that, she came willingly when I called her. Camas soon figured out that she was going to get more bird hunting experiences each day. Every night after dinner, Camas would crawl up into my lap and fall asleep, continuing to bond with me. This bonding had a lot to do with her cooperation with me in the bird field. She learned that bird hunting is a team sport between the hunter and the dog.

Asta, a six-month-old Griffon on point. photo by Glen Johnston

Your Dog's First Year in the Field

Some of the most frequently asked questions from the owners of puppies are: "What can I expect from my young dog during his first hunting season?" "How do I tell if my dog is making progress?" "When do I start using the electric collar on my pup?" The proud owner of a new pup has spent four to six months with his young dog. He has hopefully taken him for runs in the bird fields and has introduced him to the gun and birds. Pup has started to search for birds and point. The owner and his dog have bonded and become buddies. Opening day is approaching and the anticipation is great: This is going to be the best dog ever!

Here are some suggestions on what to expect from your young pup in his first season. It is important to remember that a young dog in his first year is still a juvenile. He is still growing physically, emotionally, and mentally. You should not expect a finished performance from your dog. Expect broken points, wild flushes, some chasing of birds, and inconsistencies in retrieving.

One fall a few years back, I had a visit from Barry, one of the local hunters who had purchased a male German wirehaired pointer from me. This was Barry's second dog and he was enthused and anxious to get Lars off to a good start. Barry and Lars had attended a number of our Sunday morning training sessions during the preceding summer. Lars was introduced to the gun; he was developing a field search and starting to point with intensity by the end of the summer. In October Barry traveled to eastern Montana to hunt pheasants with his dad. This was Lars' first big hunting trip at six months of age. When he returned, Barry told me that he didn't think that Lars was making the hunting progress that he should for his age. In quizzing Barry about the hunt, I found out that he and his dad got their limit of three pheasants on both days. Lars had found and pointed all of the pheasants that they shot, but he was disappointed that Lars would not retrieve the birds. He said that Lars would go to the bird but would leave it and search for more birds. I explained to Barry that he didn't really have a problem. He had a young dog with a good nose. Lars was covering the field: finding, pointing, and holding birds – a big accomplishment for a dog not even one year old. The reason he was not retrieving was his desire to find more birds. With a little backyard work that winter and the next summer, he would become a reliable retriever.

The most important thing you can accomplish during the first season is to build your dog's desire and develop his hunting ability. The most important things that you want to accomplish in your pup's first year are to develop his natural abilities: desire, use of nose, and his field search. The young dog needs to reach out and develop an animated enthusiastic search. Do not call your pup in or try to control his search at this stage. As your pup gets older he will learn to control his range based on the terrain and the birds. Dogs soon learn that, when they are hunting thick cover, they need to work close. They will also catch on to the need to stretch out and cover more ground when they are hunting big open country. While they are expanding their search they

Desire and hunting ability are two things you must instill in a young dog during its first season afield.

are also learning to use their nose. They learn to use the wind to their advantage. The bird contact in the first year will build your dog's desire. Each new contact will heighten his desire to find birds. His first year is a huge learning period. Your job is to get him out hunting wild birds as much as possible. I do not believe in putting controls on a dog during its first year. I want the dog to have fun and to explore and reach out and find birds. I have found that if you start too soon with whoa commands and controlling your dog, you run the risk of restraining the young dog too much. Over control, too early, might curtail your dog's ability to reach his fullest potential. You need to build your dog's confidence. He needs to run free and stretch out and reach for his limits. You can put the controls on your dog later. During the first season don't be concerned with retrieving. You can work on

Lars enthusiastically jumps after the bird, showing strong desire.

retrieving during the next summer. The important thing is letting the dog develop his nose and learning how to find the birds.

Leave the electric collar at home during your dog's first hunting season. The e-collar is another tool to teach and control your dog, but it is best left until the second season. You want your pup to range out and search for birds. The more bird contact he makes the better. Sure, you will get some flushes before you get to your dog. As the season progresses you'll find that your dog will recognize when he is into birds. He will be more cautious and there will be fewer wild flushes. You will also begin to read your dog and know when he is getting birdy. Each session in the field is a new experience and a new training opportunity. Your dog will learn from experience where to hunt to find the birds. He will learn how much pressure he can put on the birds and how close he can get. A pup must develop his own hunting style. It's best not to hunt a young dog too often with an older dog during the first season. A young dog is usually submissive, and the chances are great that when he is hunted with an older dog he will spend a great deal of time following the other dog. You want your dog to get out on his own and reach his fullest potential.

Keep in mind that your dog is going through a huge learning curve from kindergarten to high school in one season. Bird hunting with a dog is a team sport. You and

Barry praising Lars.

your bird dog work closely together as a unit. The better you understand your dog and the better he is able to read your wishes the better your team will be. This is your opportunity to really learn what your new dog is all about. It's called reading your dog. It's amazing how many bird hunters have trouble reading what their dog is doing.

Every dog is different. As mentioned earlier, I kept and trained three females from the same litter several years ago. It amazed me the differences in personalities and hunting techniques of each dog, even though they all had the same early training and socialization. Spend your time in the field watching your dog. Learn the signs he gives off when he starts getting birdy: he might put his head down, he often will increase his pace, and his tail might start to go faster. Watch his points; look at where his head is pointing. When you flush the bird, observe how far the bird is in front of your dog. Dogs will often point differently depending on how close they are to the bird. When Belle is right on top of the bird she is in a low crouch with her belly almost touching the ground. I can tell whether or not the birds are running just by the way Hershey is pointing. As she has been trained, Hershey holds her point until you command her to relocate. I found out that when I give Hershey the *alright* command, which is my command to relocate, she will stay on point and make one quick circle with her tail if she has the birds pinned. That's her way of telling me, "I've got them nailed down, now if you can only hit them!"

One of the problems that hunters with new dogs run into is their human hunting partners' lack of understanding about what they are trying to accomplish with the young puppy. Too often a hunting partner is concerned with getting a limit of birds and gets upset when a dog flushes them, or when the dog fails to retrieve. You need to explain to your hunting partners what you are trying to accomplish with your dog. Ask them for their help and support. If your hunting partners continue to have a problem in hunting with a young dog, perhaps it would be best to split up in the field and hunt separately.

When your dog goes on point, approach him from an angle so he can see you coming. Be careful not to shoot over his head and do not shoot more than twice. Many a young dog has become gun sensitive or gun shy by having two or three hunters shooting three-shot automatics over them in the first year. Imagine the sound of six shots or more going off in a matter of two or three seconds over your head. Remember, a dog's hearing is much more acute then a human's. You can magnify the sound you hear by at least three-fold.

There's an old saying that practice makes perfect. The more days you spend hunting and the more bird contact your dog makes during the first season, the faster he will progress in his ability. I like to extend my regular bird season with frequent hunts at a shooting preserve. The shooting preserves in most states are open until the end of March. They are a perfect way to get in some late season training after your pup's first hunting season has been completed.

My golden rule with a new pup is that he can do no wrong in his first season. I want his hunting experience to be 100% positive. Make sure that you give your dog lavish praise when he finds birds, and every time he does something right. Keep your commands to a minimum. Constantly talking to or yelling at your dog will only confuse him. My best dogs have been allowed to hunt unencumbered. They have developed their own abilities. With praise and positive reinforcement, your pup will learn how to cover a bird field, find birds, point, and retrieve on his own.

It's great to take a young dog out hunting and watch him as he goes through the field. What a thrilling sight and experience to see your dog nail his first bird and hold it until you get there to flush the bird. That's what hunting is all about. Have fun with your new pup and your first fall together!

Annie with seven-month-old pups on point in the North Dakota grasslands.

Hershey on intense point.

Use of Nose

A bird dog can have a stylish point, great drive, and be a reliable retriever, but if he doesn't have a nose, he won't be a good bird dog. A quality nose and the ability to use it well is the most important characteristic that a bird dog possesses. Fortunately most hunting dogs have a good nose. It is hard for us to totally understand the phenomenal quality of a dog's nose. The olfactory membrane in the brain is what determines the sense of smell. Dogs have olfactory membranes that are more than twice as large as humans.

Use of nose is a very hard thing to judge and one of the most difficult attributes to evaluate, mainly because we lack the understanding about scent and how it works. We can only guess what and how our dogs scent game. While the vast majority of dogs are born with a good nose, it is a physical attribute that is hard to change. You can't give your dog a nose transplant to improve what he has inherited. But, you can work with your pup and help him develop his nose to it's fullest potential. You do this by exposing your dog to birds.

When a puppy is born it cannot see or hear. However, it can smell. Watch week-old pups in the litter box with mom. They find their mom by smelling her. You can often get an idea of how good a pup's nose is by how quickly he finds mom. A pup with a good nose will be one of the first to locate mom and a nipple.

This sequence shows a nine-week-old pup pointing. Note that at first his nose is high in the air. He is not sure where the bird is. Next he lowers his head and zero's in on the bird. Finally, his nose pinpoints the bird and he locks on point.

The best way to develop your dog's nose is to get him into planted birds and then wild birds as often as possible. Remember, it takes birds to make a bird dog. In addition to birds, you will need a bird field to work your pup. I use two sizes of bird fields in training young pups. When I first introduce my pups to birds at eight to ten weeks of age, I use a small field of two to five acres. After the pup is older, I like to use a larger field of twenty to one hundred acres. Both bird fields should have good vegetation and cover in which to plant birds. I prefer cover that is ankle to knee high. You want to simulate the actual hunting conditions as much as possible. You can use quail, pigeons, chukars, or pheasants. I like to start a young pup on quail because they are small birds that give off a lot of scent. A large pigeon or pheasant might very well intimidate a young pup. I plant a quail in the grass and then bring the pup up to the edge of the field. I let pup have his head and release him with a command to *hunt 'em up*. I want pup to learn to search the area on his own. Watch your dog closely, and see how he uses his nose. Note when your dog first scents the bird. How far away was he when he first reacted to the bird's scent? The further away the pup is from the bird when he first scents it, the better his nose. A dog with a good nose will hunt into the wind. If you are working a bird field with the wind behind you, an experienced dog will run out and then work back toward you with the wind in his face. Your pup will learn to do this the more time he has in the bird field. Watch what the pup does after he first makes bird contact. Dogs with weaker noses will indicate but be unsure of exactly where the bird is located. The dog with a good nose will quickly stop when acknowledging the scent, and either point or go directly to the bird.

An eight-month-old GWP pointing at a great distance in a large field.

HERE ARE SOME THINGS TO LOOK FOR WHEN YOUR YOUNG DOG IS IN THE BIRD FIELD.

- How rapidly does the dog locate scent? Does he struggle to find the exact location or does he immediately locate the bird?
- How many times does the dog constantly find game? Is he able to find game under a variety of conditions: cross wind, down wind, no wind, high cover, etc.? The dog that finds game every time probably has a better nose than the dog that has one or two good finds and then struggles with several poor finds.
- Does the dog discriminate between old and new scent? A dog that finds a bird and points quickly has a better nose than a dog that false points or is unable to work quickly through old scent.
- How far away does the dog acknowledge game? The further away, the better the dog's nose. My dog Chukar will point his birds at a great distance; sometimes as far away as one hundred yards. You can tell by the intensity of his point how far the birds are in front of him.
- Does the dog immediately determine the direction of the bird scent? When a dog hits ground scent, is he able to figure out which way the bird is going or does he follow a back track a great distance before he figures out the bird's direction? Obviously, a dog that quickly figures out the bird's direction has a better nose than a dog that constantly backtracks.

Watch your pup's development in the field. A dog with a good nose will quickly learn from his beginning mistakes. He will pick up scent sooner and will gain confidence in locating the birds. Learn to read your dog. Watch his head and body movements. His actions will telegraph to you when he smells a bird. When a dog smells the scent cone of a bird, he will often indicate it by raising his head and breathing in scent. He probably will come to a stop and point, turning into the direction of the bird. All these signs will tell you how your pup is using his nose to find birds.

Next, for my expanded fieldwork, I like to use a twenty- to one hundred-acre field with plenty of cover. Your pup is bigger now and bolder. He should have no problem working a larger field. In this exercise, I want to develop both the dog's nose and his desire and his ability to search. Plant two to three birds in the field. When I plant birds I put a bright piece of tape on the brush near where I have planted the bird. I want to know exactly where the bird is so I can evaluate how far away my pup is when he first smells the bird, and how he handles it. When my pup is finding the birds quickly I will start to plant the birds further out in the field. Now my pup knows there are birds in the field. He should start to get really charged up and attack the bird field. At this point, I want to stretch out his field search. I also want to vary the conditions by planting the birds so the dog has to work in a crosswind and also a downwind situation. I want my dog to learn how to use the wind to his advantage at all times. A good dog will soon learn that, in a downwind situation, he has to run out a distance and work back into the wind and toward the handler. When your dog has started to do this, he is well on his way to maximizing his use of nose.

If possible, try to get your young dog into wild birds during the hunting season. As soon as the season starts, I work my young dog exclusively on wild birds. It's the best way for a young dog to learn quickly and to develop his ability to become a great dog. With wild birds, he is now playing in the big league. There is no human scent on the birds and they will be far more difficult to find. Be patient. Your dog will soon figure out the difference between tame birds and wild birds. Each encounter with wild birds will increase your dog's confidence and ability to handle them, and that ability will be enhanced by experience.

An exceptional dog is one that can tell when a covey of birds is ready to fly. He will point them from a distance and not crowd them. He also knows when to point a crippled bird, holding him there until you arrive and get a chance for a second shot. The same dog knows when a cripple cannot fly, and he will go in and retrieve the bird. Dogs with exceptional noses and intensity seldom make the mistake of flushing a bird that can still fly or of remaining on point on a bird that cannot fly.

The training exercises can be used on both young pups and adult dogs. We encourage you to spend the spring and summer working your dogs on birds. Your dogs need a summer training camp before season, just like the pro baseball players. If you are looking to buy a pup, look for a breeder who has a proven breeding program and who hunts his own dogs on wild birds at least fifty days a year. There is a great deal of difference between a dog's ability to handle preserve birds or the birds in trials and the ability to handle wild birds.

Waterwork with ducks is an excellent training method to help develop your dog's nose. After your dog has had experience on birds in the field, you can further develop his use of nose by having him search for a duck in the water. You can use several wing-clipped ducks on a pond of three acres or more with a lot of vegetation. Make sure that you pull the feathers out of only one wing. A wing-clipped duck cannot fly; however it can swim, dive under water, and walk. Good surrounding cover is a must, because you want the duck to be able to hide in the pond out of sight of your dog. You want your dog to have to use his nose, not his eyes, to locate the duck. The vegetation gives the duck a place to hide and it will also hold the duck's scent. Throw the duck into the water and let him swim away, out of sight. When the duck disappears, bring your pup up and give him a command to search for the duck. The first time or two you might want to have your pup watch as the duck swims out of sight. Then release him to find the duck. After a time or two of seeing the duck swim away your dog will know the drill; he will go out and search for the duck without seeing it released. Ideally your pup should go out into the water and cover the pond using his nose to scent and find the duck. The duck scent will stay on top of the water and on the vegetation. Watch your dog and you will see him turn in the direction of where the duck swam when he hits the scent cone. Since you watched where the duck went, you can tell if your dog is picking up his scent. When your dog is searching over 75% of the time with his nose and not his eyes, your dog is well on his way to using his nose properly.

Dog pounds the water searching for the duck.

Pheasant hunting with Belle.

You can build your young pups desire by using a bird wing.

Desire & Cooperation:
The Balancing Act

Desire and cooperation are two very important qualities that every good bird dog must possess in order to produce game for the hunter. Desire for a dog is his prey drive. A dog with a strong prey drive has a great never-ending desire to work. This desire is demonstrated in the dog's search for game, his intensity on point, his retrieving, and his waterwork. Every dog has a different level of desire. A dog with exceptional desire will hunt hard all day even if few or no birds are found. In fact, he will increase his drive until he finds birds. A low desire dog will quit working if he doesn't make game contact early in the day. The prey drive in a dog is genetic. It is a quality that is passed on to a puppy through his bloodlines. While it is a genetic quality, it can be awakened and strengthened by exposing a dog to birds. The best way to increase desire is to get a young dog into wild birds as often as possible.

I like to use live birds in the field to build the dog's level of desire. I start with a five- or six-week-old puppy by letting him chase a bird wing on a pole. This awakens the prey drive in a young pup. You can carry this process forward by tossing dummies to the young dog. Watch the pup that runs out and grabs the dummy and carries it around. He possesses a strong indication of a high desire and prey drive. I also use the dog's prey drive to teach it to track and recover cripples.

During hunting season, if I have a wounded bird on the ground and have a young dog in the truck with us, I will get the pup and let him track and find the live bird. A wounded live bird running ahead of the dog really builds up his enthusiasm and desire. Exposing your dog to wild birds in the field as soon as possible will develop this desire in him. I like to take my young puppies out into the hunting field in their first year, starting them in the bird field as early as twelve weeks of age. You have to be willing to give up some shooting opportunities in order to introduce your young dog to wild birds. Let your dog learn how to search the field; let him explore and work out the bird scent. Sure he will flush birds. Go ahead and let him chase them. With each bird contact, your dog will be building his desire and confidence and learning how to search, find, and ultimately hold wild birds. When you train dogs, it is their prey drive that keeps them working even when they have to face many corrections in their training lessons. A dog with strong desire can overcome many mediocre qualities and still be an excellent hunter. The dog that lacks desire will frequently let his owner down. There is a great deal of frustration and disappointment when you own a dog that just doesn't have the desire to reach out and hunt hard-to-find birds.

A duck chase is another great way to build desire in a young dog. Take a duck and either clip one wing or tape both wings to its body. Now the duck cannot fly but it can still swim, dive under water and, if it gets back on the land, it can walk and hide. Bring your dog up to the edge of a small pond or marsh. Show him the duck. While you are holding your dog, have a helper throw the duck out into the water and let your dog go

Yogi nails a valley quail.

after the duck. You can also use multiple dogs for this exercise. Using multiple dogs builds up a competitive spirit that builds desire. The dogs will leap out into the water and race each other to see who can catch the duck first. This is a great way to take a dog with low desire and bring him up to speed.

A dog with a high desire level will exhibit this in the way it hunts birds. When hunting wild birds you will have times when you and your dog will not make bird contact for a long period of time. A dog with low desire will shut down his search after a period of time with no bird contact. On the other hand, a high desire dog will be searching even harder the longer he goes without bird contact. He believes that there are birds in the field. He will stretch out and search until he finds them. Hunting in thick cover and plowing through it is another example of a high desire dog. We have all seen dogs that refuse to work tough cover. Tough cover does not stop the high desire dog.

Cooperation is the willingness of the dog to work for you and the gun. Hunting is a team sport. You take the dog to the field you want him to hunt; it's his job to find the birds. This is where desire comes into play. He finds the birds, points them, and holds point until you come up, flush the bird, and shoot.

Your dog's pointing and steadiness to shot is the cooperation part of the equation. If he lacks cooperation, he will take the bird out rather than holding point and letting you flush and shoot the bird. Cooperation is not as essential as desire, because an uncooperative dog can be controlled with obedience training. The dog that lacks desire cannot be forced to do something in which he has no interest. Desire is the most important quality. Without desire, you cannot reach the point where cooperation becomes important.

Desire and cooperation both compliment each other and at times they may be at odds with each other. Both qualities come in varying degrees in each dog. There is no black and white, only a range of varying degrees of gray. The ideal situation is to have a dog with very strong desire, and yet one who wants to work with his hunter and be very cooperative. Achieving both high desire and cooperation in your dog is a balancing act. Every action of a hunting dog is a combination of these two qualities. When a dog searches the field, he is showing desire. When he holds point and lets you flush and shoot the bird, he is showing cooperation. When the dog tracks and retrieves a wounded bird, he is showing desire; and when he brings the bird to you, he is showing cooperation.

All dog owners should strive to develop both qualities in their dogs and achieve a balance between the two qualities. Dogs with strong prey drives are sometimes slower to work with their handlers. They charge into the field and are focused on finding birds. They normally are strong runners and cover a lot of ground. They are on the edge and hunting for themselves. It will take longer for this type of dog to learn to cooperate with its hunter. My male, Chukar, was a handful his first two hunting seasons. He had a very strong prey drive and spent little time checking back with me. He had all the genetic hunting tools; they just weren't in the toolbox. I found that after I whoa trained him and force broke him to retrieve he handled better. He began to learn that bird hunting was a team sport. When Chukar was a puppy he was not much interested in being held or patted, he was too interested in playing and exploring. Chukar, like all of our dogs, spends time each day in our home. He also goes to the office with us several times a week. Over the two-year period his personality changed. He bonded with Blanche and I and now wanted to please us. Chukar really matured in his third season. He still ranged out and covered the ground. However, now he would swing by and check on where we were. When he got into birds he would point them and hold them until we got to him. During one hunt I lost track of Chukar. He had gone over a hill. I called for him and he did not come. When I went over the hill I saw him on point. He knew to hold point even though I had made the mistake of calling. It took me five minutes to reach him. I flushed a covey of Huns and killed two. Chukar retrieved the birds and we continued our hunt. Now Chukar and I hunt together as a team. I seldom use the whistle. I know where he is even when I can't see him. He also knows to check back with me. If he doesn't, I know he is on point and I go looking for him. I have even had occasions when Chukar has come back to me and looked at me as if to say, "Follow me. I know where the birds are." He will turn and trot ahead a few yards and look back at me to see if I am following him. He then leads me to the birds and goes back on point. Every dog develops its hunting skills over a different length of time, some more slowly than others. Be patient and continue to work with your dog. It took Chukar three years to get it together, now he has all of the tools in the toolbox. He is the finest bird dog I have ever had.

Several seasons ago I was hunting chukars with Jeff Funke and Jim Tenuto. At the end of the day we spotted a covey of chukars on a rocky slope near the jeep trail. We stopped our rig and Jeff let out Aggie, one of his German wirehaired pointers. Aggie went over to the rock cliff and locked on point. We climbed the cliff and came over the top, catching the birds by surprise. We knocked three birds down on the flush. Aggie quickly retrieved one of the dead birds. The other two birds were winged, and we saw both of them running away through the sagebrush. Aggie started tracking one of the birds as I went back to the truck to let Belle, Chukar's mother and my wirehair, down. I took Belle over to where the birds fell and told her to *hunt dead*. It took her several minutes to find the track of the one wounded bird, but soon she was hot on the trail. She started moving quickly with her nose to the ground. We watched her track the bird across the sagebrush for over 700 yards. Finally, she disappeared over the hill. I stood and waited for over five minutes. Then she appeared coming back at a run with the bird in her mouth. She proudly brought the bird to me. When we got back to the truck and drove out, I measured the distance that Belle had tracked the bird. It was over half a mile from where she started tracking the chukar to where she disappeared over the hill. I have no idea how much further she went before she caught the wounded bird. Belle's strong desire motivated her to track a bird she did not see, and her desire to please me and work with me resulted in her bringing the bird back and delivering it to me.

Yogi shows great desire and cooperation with this duck retrieve.

Good breeding and a solid temperament are the keys to bringing out the qualities of desire and cooperation and to developing the balance of these qualities in your dog. In my opinion, early socialization of your puppy and bonding with him are the most important factors in creating a normal temperament in a dog. Early socialization makes a bold high-desire dog and bonding makes a cooperative dog. Socialization starts at three to four weeks of age. As soon as a puppy opens its eyes, it can relate to people. The critical period is from three weeks to sixteen weeks. A young puppy needs to have human contact and learn to relate to and interact with people. A young dog should also be exposed to the outside world. Riding in cars, taking walks, meeting strangers; all of these exposures will build your pup's confidence and self-esteem. You want a puppy with a solid temperament. When you get your young puppy, make sure that you continue to accelerate the socialization process.

Start bonding with your puppy the day you get him. Let him ride in the car with you back from the kennel or the airport. Hold him in your lap. Bring him into the house and make him a part of the family. Take him with you on all of your outings: cross-country skiing, fishing, hiking, running, etc. This is your buddy. You want your dog to regard you as the most important person in his life. You want him to be totally devoted to you and your family. When you have a puppy that is well socialized and devoted to you, you will have a dog that has a good prey desire coupled with the will to want to please you. That means cooperating with you. Try this approach and you will be amazed at the results.

Tom Lally, a hunter from Washington State, bought a male puppy from me a few years ago. Tom hadn't had a bird dog for over twenty years. He admitted that he didn't know much about training a dog. I advised him to do four things for his young pup. Bring him into the family, continue the socialization that we started, and bond with him. Finally, get him out into the wild bird field and put him into as many wild birds as possible. Don't worry about him making mistakes. Let him learn and have fun. Tom followed my advice. He took his puppy, Yogi, everywhere with him. He had Yogi in the house every day, playing and spending time with his family. Tom and his young son took Yogi out hunting every weekend during hunting season. They did not expect a finished dog the first season. They were patient and allowed Yogi to explore, learning how to search and find birds. Yes, Yogi made mistakes; he flushed birds, chased them, and did all the other transgressions of youth. However, each hunt Yogi got better, he gained more confidence and started to figure out how to find and handle wild birds. He was having fun. Right after Thanksgiving I got an e-mail from Tom:

"Hi Chuck and Blanche - Yogi grew up today and am I ever relieved. My son and I went hunting a river bottom area and Yogi searched the area and found and pointed five pheasants. He retrieved the three pheasants that we hit. One of them was wounded and he had to track the bird for a good ten minutes before he found it. He retrieved the live bird to hand. The area was a public hunting spot and the birds had been pushed frequently so they didn't hold very long, but Yogi did all of the work himself. I thought I would share that bit of Thanksgiving news with you. I know that you know, but Yogi just turned six months old yesterday. For six months old I think he is fantastic."

The key to getting a dog that will have a great deal of desire and cooperation is to pick a pup from a breeder who is producing dogs that have those qualities. Then make sure that you socialize and bond with your dog and get him into plenty of birds. That's the way to develop another Yogi.

Young pups following older dogs in the field begin to learn to search and develop boldness with cover.

Developing Your Dog's Ability to Search

Searching the game field and finding birds for the hunter is one of the most important abilities a pointing dog must possess. The difference between an excellent day in the field with birds in the game bag and a mediocre day with few or no bird opportunities for the hunter is dependent on the dog's ability to cover the hunting area and find birds. Many years ago, right after college when my wife Blanche and I were hunting on opening day, we spotted a cock pheasant fly into and land in a tall grass field. Before we got to the field three hunters along with their dogs entered the field and tried to find the pheasant. We stood there and watched the hunters and their dogs make a quick sweep through the field and leave without finding the bird. I turned to Blanche and said, "Well, let's go get that pheasant". She was sure that the bird had left the field, but I convinced her that we had a good chance of finding it. We entered the field with our English setter, who covered the area and pointed the cock bird. We had our first pheasant in the bag. Our setter's ability to search with desire and cooperation found the pheasant for us.

Developing a good search pattern in a dog is a complex assignment for the handler. You need a dog that has good search ability while still maintaining a cooperative

A bold pup pointing a bird in heavy cover.

As long as the dogs check back in with you and will hold birds, let them run their natural range.

link with his hunter. I like to compare the bird hunting experience in the field between a hunter and his bird dog with the pitcher and the catcher in baseball. The catcher is the hunter. He calls the game plan. The dog is the pitcher. It's his job to find the birds and point them, presenting the hunter with a good shot and an opportunity to kill the bird. Cooperation between hunter and dog is the key to success in the hunting field. No matter how big the search, the object is to point birds for the gun. A dog's search should vary depending on the bird being hunted and the terrain. Wild birds are the key to increasing the dog's desire and intensity: creating a successful search. Planted birds do not create the same desire that wild birds do. Even a young dog knows the difference between a tame, planted bird and a wild bird. Wild birds force the dog to use the wind and to expand his search. It also teaches him how to handle wild birds. The dog soon learns that he cannot crowd wild birds, as he can often do with pen-raised birds. He has to point them from a distance. A young pup that is exposed to and worked mainly on wild birds will learn how to search out the cover and hunt objectives while maintaining a cooperative link with his handler. He will develop a well-rounded search pattern and find a lot of birds. I like to put my dogs on wild birds as soon as possible. Camas only had one session with planted birds in her first season, but she had forty days hunting wild birds.

I want my dogs to be able to handle all variations of cover and terrain from wide-open grasslands to thick cover. I like my dogs to work at a faster pace in open country and slow their search pattern down in thick cover. The important element to their well-rounded search pattern is that the dog is always aware of the location and the direction of the handler.

The genetic makeup of the dog plays the most important role in the dog's overall inherent ability to develop a great search pattern. However, in training a young dog, you can influence some of the behavior. Search is a combination of range, how a dog covers the ground, how he hunts objectives, and his desire and cooperation while trying to produce game for the gun. You want a dog to search in front of you. Range is simply the distance a dog hunts from the handler. Desire is how passionately a dog goes about his search, and cooperation is the tie between the handler and the dog.

I do not specifically train a dog to run a precise pattern. Many handlers like a dog to quarter back and forth in front of the handler in a perfect Z, always staying the same distance in front of the hunter. I prefer to let each dog develop its own pattern. Each dog has a unique hunting style and if you try to change his style, you run the chance of inhibiting his search. Let your dog develop his style and search by running him on wild birds in various types of cover and terrain. Your dog will soon learn where to look for the birds. If a fault appears in your dog's pattern, you can correct it. If a dog returns to you too frequently, send the dog out again with encouragement. Do the same thing if the dog wants to work behind you. You will find that most dogs soon learn to hunt in the front and change directions as you change directions, without a command.

Each handler has a preference as to the range he wants his dog to work. A dog needs to work close in thick CRP fields while hunting pheasants or while hunting grouse in thick woods. A dog's range can vary when hunting open country for prairie birds or chukars. Most hunters like their dogs to work close at all times in all types of cover. I like our dogs to run fairly big in open country. The greater a dog's range, the greater the risk of bumped birds, disobedience, or flat out losing your dog. On the other hand, the greater the dog's range, the greater the potential return in the number of covey finds. We own pointing dogs so that we can cover the ground and find birds. The more range the better, as long as the dog remains in contact with the handler, hunts to the front, holds his birds, and remains obedient.

My dogs vary their range according to the cover and the bird. When I hunt Hershey in the woods of western Montana for ruffed grouse, she ranges only thirty to sixty yards away from me. I often hunt chukars in the morning and valley quail in the afternoon with the same dogs. My dogs range out on the chukar slopes and hunt close when we are hunting quail. I have built a cooperative bond with my dogs. They cover as much ground as possible under varying conditions while still maintaining a cooperative contact with me.

Most dogs will run a bit wild for the first ten minutes of a search. You should let your pup run this way if you want to encourage your dog to have a greater range. Have faith in your dog. To constantly hack your dog with your voice or whistle will only shorten his range and create an over-dependence on you, his handler. Or he will rebel by ignoring you and hunt for himself.

The application, the level of desire your dog has in his search, is based in large part on his inherited ability. It's in the genes. A dog lacking desire will let you down even if he has other exceptional attributes such as a good nose and strong pointing ability. Without strong desire, the nose never gets to the birds and the point is never seen. As trainer, your job in building desire is to expose your dog to as many wild birds as possible. The more chances your dog has to find birds and retrieve them the better the chances of building his desire to range out and find birds. You want a dog that will continue to search hard all day looking for birds.

Cooperation is the final ingredient in a dog's search that is necessary to put birds in your game bag. A cooperative dog works with you. He maintains contact, adjusts his range according to the terrain, and changes directions with you. The two of you work as a team. The best way to develop cooperation in your young dog is with positive training. During your pup's first months with you, spend time with him. Develop a strong bond with him. Take him with you for walks and on short and long trips. Get him out into the field with you. When your young pup loses you in the field, don't call out for him. Let him find you on his own. Once your pup learns to track you down he will always be able to find you during a hunting situation. He has learned that he needs to check back with you and depend on you.

Most uncooperative dogs have been made so by their handlers. Here are some of the common mistakes that many handlers make:

- Trying to totally control a dog's search.
- Constantly hacking and whistle blowing, so the dog starts ignoring the handler.
- Getting mad at the dog and losing your temper.
- Letting the dog run without your presence. If the dog learns that he is allowed to run free without you and find birds, he will start to self-hunt. Make sure that you are always in the hunting field with your dog.

It takes time and patience to help your dog develop a good search. Your patience and effort will allow your pup to develop his own style. Have fun and have faith in your dog. Your reward will be the thrill of watching a great dog search the field and pin birds for you.

Cedarwoods Delta Dawn, a Pudelpointer on point in chukar country.
photo by Bob Farris

These young pups show their natural pointing instinct by pointing one another.

Introducing Your Dog to Birds and Developing the Pointing Instinct

There is no more thrilling sight to a bird dog hunter than his pointing dog standing in the field on intense point. Pointing for a dog is a natural instinct that is present in varying degrees in all hunting dogs. It is the pause before the pounce. Watch how a coyote hunts. It pauses and stands rigid just before it pounces on it prey. A fox will act the same way when it is hunting for food.

Over the course of centuries, hunters have developed that pointing instinct in their dogs. Heredity plays a major part in a dog's pointing ability. There is evidence of pointing dogs as early as the Twelfth Century in Spain. These dogs were referred to as Spanish pointers. Through the selective breeding process, the pointing response has been developed over the years to a high degree of intensity and duration; resulting in today's modern pointers who remain totally motionless, standing like statues, until their prey moves. This is a natural pointing instinct.

All pointers are not created equal. Some dogs have too much point and will lock up on strange objects or old scent. This is often an indication of a poor nose. Other dogs have too little pointing instinct. They often fail to point a bird and often flush a wild bird, depriving the hunter of a chance at a shot. The overall quality of your dog's pointing instinct has a direct correlation to how successful you will be at hunting wild birds.

You can break down pointing into three segments: speed, intensity, and duration. Pointing speed is defined as how quickly a dog locks up or stops on point upon first smelling bird scent. There is a notable difference in the way dogs handle their first bird scent. Some dogs slow down and creep up close to the bird before they point. It is great to see a dog that locks up immediately once he scents the bird. Wild birds do not wait for a dog to lock up on point. They will often flush when a dog attempts to creep up on them. It is better to have an overly cautious dog that can be relocated than a dog that pushes the birds. If the birds are pushed, they will be gone and you won't get a chance for a shot. You can tell a dog that has spent most of its time hunting preserve birds. These dogs have a tendency to push the birds and get up close before they point. Preserve birds do not act the same as wild birds. They will often let a dog push them, without taking flight. A dog that has spent most of its time hunting preserve birds will have a relearning process when you hunt him on wild birds. A good dog will soon learn that he cannot push a wild bird.

Pointing intensity is the rigid posture of the dog's body and the passionate expression on his face. A dog with an intense point will have his eyes bright and focused, his muscles will quiver and his whole body will be rock solid. A dog that lacks intensity will wag his tail and move his head or shift his body. He will be far less focused on the bird.

Using a wing to get an indication of your pups pointing instinct.

Pointing duration is the length of time that a dog will remain locked on point. We are not talking about steadiness here; we are talking about pointing with intensity for an extended period of time. A dog with great pointing ability will remain on point and motionless and not flush the bird, even if it takes you five to ten minutes to reach him.

The year we kept the three pups, Hershey, Belle, and Sprig, from one litter, we had an opportunity to observe an interesting phenomenon. We would often observe the three pups pointing each other while playing in the yard. One of the dogs would start to point the other. Soon all three of them would be facing each other in staunch points. I clocked them several times. They would stand pointing each other for five minutes or more. All three had intense points and no one wanted to be the first dog to break point. Since that time, I have observed a number of my dogs pointing each other as part of their game playing. I tell people that my dogs are practicing pointing, just like you would practice shooting or go to a golf driving range to practice your golf swing.

Many people use a bird wing on a pole to judge a dog's interest in birds. I like to use the wing to evaluate a pup's pointing ability. The way a pup points the wing is a good indication of its pointing instinct. Toss the wing out and watch your pup. The pup that locks up immediately has a great deal of inherited pointing ability. Watch how intense and focused your pup is. Intensity is the key. If a pup does not point a wing, it does not mean that he will not develop into a good pointer. Every dog develops at a different pace. Your pup might be too immature, or lack a strong desire for prey. However, the young puppy that points a wing with speed, intensity, and duration, will always be a strong pointer. Use the wing on a pole to test your dog's pointing instinct. After you have observed his interest in pointing, discontinue using the wing on a pole. Change to live birds. You want your dog to point scent, not point by sight.

When a pup is nine or ten weeks old you can plant a quail or chukar in the field and then bring your pup into the field downwind of the bird. Do not use a check cord. Let your pup roam the field and find the bird on his own. Watch your pup. This is a good time to judge his nose. Many times your pup will not scent-point the bird, because he is not sure what it is. After your dog points the bird he will probably dive in and flush it. When the bird starts to fly your pup will chase it. This will build his prey drive. Your dog will soon learn he cannot catch the birds and should start locking up tight at the scent. If your dog does well at this exercise, he is sure to be a strong pointer.

Mistakes in early training are the biggest detriment to developing your dog's pointing instinct. All of us have seen dog owners do more to inhibit their dog's pointing instinct than they do to develop it. The standard scenario is a training session where the owner puts out a hobbled bird in the field, puts a check cord on his dog, and then leads him up to the bird while holding on to the check cord. What has the handler done wrong? First, he restrained the dog, inhibiting his ability to learn how to search and use his nose to find the bird. Second, he taught the dog that the bird would stay on the ground and not move even though the dog is lunging at it. The dog soon thinks he can catch the bird as soon as he is off the lead.

You can use several methods to develop your dog's pointing ability. The first and best method involves working your dog on wild birds. Wild birds will not let your dog get close or pressure them. Your dog will soon learn that he can't catch the bird and will start pointing. This is really the most ideal way to develop a really intense point on your young dog. I want my young dogs to train on wild birds as soon as possible. On opening day, I have my young pups, even ones that are only fourteen to sixteen weeks old, in the field hunting wild birds. Once I start hunting them on wild birds I do not use any pen-raised birds. All of my dogs' bird contact will be on wild birds for the duration of the hunting season. By hunting wild birds, my young pup will accelerate his hunting ability.

Another method is to use automatic bird releases. You can use any variety of birds: such as quail, chukars, or pigeons. Pigeons are the cheapest birds to use and, if you get homing pigeons, you can use them over and over again. Try to create an environment as close to hunting wild birds as possible. I like to plant two to three birds in automatic bird launchers that I have placed throughout the training field. I start my pup into the field with a crosswind. As soon as the dog scents a bird, I am ready to launch the bird out of the trap if the pup looks as if he is not going to point. At this stage I do not want the dog to chase the bird. The dog has to learn that he must stop and point as soon as he first scents the bird. I do not want him to get a reward by chasing the bird. When the dog starts to point, I stand back and watch the dog. I let the dog build his pointing duration and learn that as long as he remains on point, the bird will not flush. As soon as the dog loses intensity or starts to advance, I launch

Cedarwoods Neon Playgirl a pudelpointer with a beautiful intense point. photo by Bob Farris

the bird. As the sessions advance and the dog extends his pointing time, I approach the dog until I am at his side. I then gently push the dog toward the bird from his rear haunches. The dog's normal reaction is to resist and become more intense. It is important during these sessions to give no commands. Remain silent; we are developing the pup's natural pointing ability, not training for steadiness. Steadiness is a trained command, pointing is an instinct. Pointing and steadiness should be trained separately. By allowing your dog to stand on point for several minutes uninterrupted, you are building cooperation and a sense of teamwork. You are starting to build an invisible link between you and your dog.

With an automatic release trap, you can flight the bird when the dog has not scented it or seen it. The dog doesn't have a clue the bird is there. This simulates a typical scenario in wild bird hunting. Many times a dog is on the wrong side of the wind and flushes a bird he does not know is there. By using an occasional automatic, you are keeping your dog on his toes, and teaching him to be cautious and focused. All of these methods are employed in developing your dog's pointing instinct. However, the most important method is to get your dog into wild birds in the game field as soon as possible, understanding that, in the beginning, your main goal is to train your dog, not to fill your game bag. You will be able to enjoy many days of full game bags and wonderful dog work, if you take the time to develop your dog into the best he can be.

Judy Balogs's Weimaraner, Gunnar, on point. photo by Judy Balog

Baron's first duck.

Waterwork:
Introducing Your Young Pup to the Water

Hunters are attracted to the versatile breeds of dogs because they have a great ability to find and point upland birds, along with a love of water, and an ability to track and find wounded game. They can do it all and do it well. Owning a dog that loves the water and will swim out and retrieve birds is not only important for a waterfowl hunter, but also for the upland hunter. Several times a year I end up shooting a pheasant that falls across a creek or into a river or lake. Without a dog that is willing to go into the water to retrieve the bird, that bird would be lost.

Many versatile breeds possess a genetic love of water. If you want a dog that has a strong disposition toward water, get one from a breeder whose dogs love the water. We have developed a strong water desire in our line of dogs. We introduce our dogs to the water at an early age. You want to prepare your pup for water retrieving by exposing him to water in a positive manner, so that he is confident and bold when the time comes for serious waterwork. Make sure that the weather is warm and the water temperature is pleasant for a young dog. You want his first experiences to be fun and confidence building.

When we have a litter of pups, we start taking them out into the field at five weeks of age. The area we use has a small spring creek that runs through the property. The

Pups at the waters edge watch their mom swim across the stream.

Encourage your pup to brave the water.

creek is fifteen to twenty feet wide and shallow on both sides. The middle of the creek is about knee deep. We run the puppies with their mother and the other older dogs. The puppies love to follow and chase the older dogs. After they have had a short run and are warm from running, we cross the creek, and call the pups, encouraging them to follow us. The older dogs jump into the creek and set an example. Often the pups will leap into the water and follow us without even realizing that they are in water for the first time. Occasionally one or two of the pups will hesitate and stay on the other side of the creek. When this happens, we start playing with the older dogs and the puppies that have already crossed the creek, lavishing praise on them. The puppies on the other side are eager to be with their mom and littermates and jealous of the attention that they are getting. Soon they will enter the water and cross the creek. They are able to walk part way and they only have to swim a short distance. They can see the other side and soon they are back in shallow water where they can stand. We lavish praise on each puppy when it goes into the water and when it reaches the other side.

We take our puppies and older dogs out at least twice a week. After two or three times in the field the puppies will plunge into the water on their own. I introduce my pups to birds at the same age as I introduce them to water. I also start them on retrieving dummies. Puppies love to retrieve. It is a great game for them. Once you have your puppy running out and retrieving a dummy on land it is easy to make the transition to water retrieves.

One pup takes the plunge!

These hesitant pups finally got jealous of the excitement on the other side and decided to see just what the water was made of.

After a few weeks of swimming across a small stream, I put the pups and the older dogs on a chain gang by a small pond. I start by throwing dummies for the older dogs. The young pup will get excited and pull on the chain for his turn. When I let the pup off of the chain and throw a dummy into the water for him, he will usually plunge right in and swim out to retrieve it. I start by throwing the dummy only a few feet into the water. As the pup's enthusiasm and confidence increases I will increase the length of the water retrieve.

I also use dead pigeons and ducks when I am teaching my young pup to retrieve. A young pup of only four weeks will start to retrieve small dummies. When he is about eight to ten weeks and retrieving has become a great game for him, I start using dead birds. After he is retrieving dead birds on land, it is easy to get him to go into the water and retrieve them. Camas started going into the shallow water to retrieve a dead duck at ten weeks of age.

Here are some tips and techniques to use if you have a puppy that is hesitant about going into the water. Most importantly, never get mad and try to force a puppy into the water. One of the easiest methods to get a pup excited about the water is to use the bird wing on a pole. Take the pup to the edge of the water and start to excite him and get him chasing the wing. When he is really chasing the wing, move it out over shallow water. Most pups want the wing so bad that they will forget about the water and wade in to get the wing. Eventually you can work the dog into the water. Let him catch the wing, expanding the process until the pup is swimming a short distance to catch it. When your pup is going readily into the water after the wing, you can proceed with the other steps in introducing him to the water.

You can also use a wing-clipped pigeon. Show it to your puppy without getting it so close to him that he can grab it. This will get him excited. When he is lunging to catch the bird, throw it out a short distance into the water. Your pup will often jump into the water and swim out to catch and retrieve the bird. In this case the dog's prey drive will overcome his fear of the water.

Another great method to get a reluctant puppy to love the water is to take along a few dogs, either older dogs or puppies that love the water. Tape the wings of a live duck so that it cannot fly. The duck will still be able to swim and walk. Put all but one of the dogs on a chain gang. Throw the duck out into the water and let one of the dogs chase the duck. The dogs on the chain gang will start barking and lunging on the chain, trying to get loose to chase the duck. Let another dog that loves the water loose and let him join the chase. Let all of the dogs except the hesitant one join in the chase. When the action builds to a crescendo you now have puppies having a ball chasing the duck and one pup agonizing on the chain trying to get into the game. Finally turn the hesitant pup loose and let him have fun chasing the duck with the other dogs.

It is a great thrill to hunt over a dog that loves the water and can match or exceed the ability of a retriever. You have a truly versatile dog that excels at hunting upland birds and waterfowl, a dog that does it all and does it well.

This eight-week-old pup shows a strong natural desire to retrieve.

Developing Your Dog into a Natural Retriever

There are many dogs that are natural retrievers. A natural retriever loves to retrieve, and has a high desire to find the birds and bring them back to his handler. Developing natural retrieving is the process of utilizing your pup's inherited natural instincts along with the bond that you have created with your pup, to build a hunting dog that will retrieve shot game to hand willingly. I believe that the work a dog does after the shot is every bit as important as the work before the shot. The hunting situation is not complete until the shot bird is brought to hand. Dogs that don't have a high desire to retrieve must be force broke. Force breaking is a controlled negative training process whereby the dog is subjected to ear pinching, a nerve hitch on his toe, or use of the electric collar to make the dog pick up the dummy, hold it, and retrieve it. It is not true that you must force break all dogs to insure that they are dependable retrievers. Many dogs are natural retrievers, as most of my dogs have been. However, I force break all of my dogs after they are at least a year old and have had one full hunting season with them. My reason is that even a dependable natural retriever will sometimes refuse to retrieve. I want to make sure that I can enforce retrieving under any circumstance. I have also found that the discipline used in the force break or trained retrieve sessions helps in the whoa training sessions. Once your young dog knows that he has to retrieve for you every time, you have established control over him and you have set the tone for all future training sessions.

The dog that will develop into a great natural retriever has those inherited qualities passed on to him from his parents, grandparents, and great-grandparents. When you are selecting a puppy look at the ancestors. Ask the breeder and the owners of pups from that breeder, how their dogs retrieve: Are they natural retrievers? A young pup that likes to pick up an object and carry it around is a good candidate to develop into a great retriever. Dogs with a strong prey drive also have the desire to make difficult water retrieves and run down the mountains two to three hundred yards to pick up the crippled chukar that flew down the steep slope to the bottom. Look for a pup that possesses a strong prey drive when selecting your puppy.

As soon as you bring your pup home with you, it is time to begin developing his instinct to retrieve. You will need the following items:

- soft play toys,
- small dummies to begin with and,
- larger dummies later,
- a long lead, and finally
- frozen and live birds.

Make your sessions short, no more than five to ten minutes, and no more than twice a day. If you set up your training sessions right, your pup will regard it as play time. He will not even be aware that you are training him. Stack the deck in your favor. Always have a purpose when you are training. Start your training in a comfortable area that is familiar to your pup. It's best to start the sessions in your home. When you are working with your pup do not let him romp with other pets or people. While the early sessions will appear as playtime to your pup, you have a definite purpose and goal to reach. Start by tossing a soft object, such as a play toy, a few feet in front of your pup. His prey drive should cause him to give chase and pick up the toy. When he picks it up, clap your hands and use your voice to encourage him to bring it to you. When your pup comes near you, pet him and praise him. Do not take the toy away from him immediately. The mistake many people make is to take the toy, dummy, or bird out of the dog's mouth too soon. Remember, that strong prey drive causes your dog to want to possess the object or bird in his mouth. Letting him hold it is part of his reward for bringing it back to you. Along with receiving praise from you, it is the only reward he will get for retrieving. When hunting with my older dogs I also let them hold the dead bird for a couple of minutes if they want to. I put my arm around them, petting them and praising them softly. You will soon learn when your dog is ready to let the bird go. At that time give him your release command and gently take the bird out of his mouth.

Keep these retrieving toys separate from your pup's other toys. Keep them for use during your training sessions only; you want the retrieving toys to spark excitement in your dog. After a few sessions your dog will get excited when you bring out the dummies. He will begin to anticipate these training sessions. Once you have an excited eager pup, the training will go much faster. If your pup gets tired or does not want to cooperate with you during the training sessions, stop and put him up. He will soon learn that the fun stops when he does not cooperate with you.

Your pup will not always bring the toy back to you. Don't worry about this at this early stage. Just make sure you praise your pup every time he does bring the toy to you and he will soon learn that it is more fun to bring it to you. Gradually make the retrieves longer by tossing the toy out farther. Start using a command when you throw the toy. Say, *Fetch* or whatever command you intend to use. The word is not important. What is important is consistency. Pick a word and stick with it. When your pup brings the toy back to you and is ready to release it, pick another command for the release: *Give, Drop,* etc. Again, pick one word and be consistent. If your pup does not come to you after some coaxing, do not get mad. Move to another area of the house. I like to use a hallway. With an enclosed area the pup has only one way to go; he can only run back to you. If your pup is reluctant to give you the dummy after you have let him hold it and have given him praise, do not tear it from his mouth. Take hold of his collar and use your release command. Most pups will drop the dummy. As a last resort you can pinch his flank while giving the command. Make sure that you throw the dummy again as soon as your pup drops it. He will soon learn that the game only continues if he gives you the dummy.

In the next stage, move your training to a larger area. Go outside into the yard. If you have a fenced area in your yard, so much the better. The fenced area will control the dog's ability to run away with the dummy. Once you move outside, you may need to keep your pup on a long lead for a while. Do not jerk or pull on the lead. Use the lead to steer your pup to the dummy or to bring him back to you. I have a long deck around the front of my house. I like to use it at this stage. The pup is outside and

I can give him a long toss and retrieve. However, he still has only one way to go; he can only run back to me. After he is consistently bringing the dummy back to me, I move into the fenced yard.

Praise your dog and let him hold the bird for a couple of minutes.

After your dog is retrieving well, hold him by the collar, throw the dummy, and do not let him go after it until you give him the retrieve command. Later on, after your pup is whoa broke, you will want your dog to associate your retrieve command as his release to retrieve. Start by holding your pup until the dummy hits the ground. Gradually, hold your pup for a longer time, until he learns to wait for the retrieve command. At this stage continue to expand the length of the retrieves as well as making

This pup hits the water with enthusiasm for retrieves.

them more difficult. Throw the dummy into tall grass. Use different areas and different terrain. Your dog will have to retrieve over all kinds of cover and now is the time to expose him to it.

Hopefully you will have introduced your puppy to water and he is swimming. If that is the case, you can start your pup on water retrieves. Begin with short tosses into the water. When your pup is eagerly going into the water and retrieving the dummy, increase the distance of your toss. Make sure that you introduce water retrieves when the water is warm. You don't want to turn your pup off to retrieving by putting him in cold water.

If you have followed these steps you should have a pretty good retriever by four to six months. Now you can introduce your pup to retrieving birds. Do not start out with warm or fresh birds. You do not want to confuse your pup. He might want to point a warm bird. Also remember the prey drive. A warm bird is a big temptation for a dog to want to chew or eat it. Use frozen birds for your early training. Since a frozen bird gives off less scent, your pup will not be as tempted to point, and he will not be able to chomp down hard on a frozen bird. He will have to carry it softly. It is best to use a long lead when you switch to birds, as your dog might want to run off with it. Start with short retrieves and go back to using a confined area, deck, or a fenced yard. When your dog is bringing the bird back to you, expand the length of the retrieve and move into more difficult cover. It is important to introduce your dog to birds when he is young. If you wait until an actual hunting situation, your dog will probably mouth and play with the bird. He will not be used to it. You want your dog to be a dependable retriever on birds before the hunting season.

Retriever people spend a lot of time teaching their dogs to mark retrieves. We can learn from them. You want your dog to watch where the bird falls. After you have a

Use a confined area to start your pups first retrieving lessons.

dependable retriever, start your marking drills. You will need an assistant to help you. Have your helper go out into the field with a dummy and a blank gun. He should start out about twenty-five to thirty yards in front of you and your dog. You hold your dog by the collar. The helper should fire the gun and at the same time throw the dummy at a right angle to the dog. Release your dog while the dummy is still in the air, using your retrieve command. To repeat the exercise have the helper move forward, perpendicular to you and your dog, so that the next throw is over fresh ground. When your dog starts to watch the helper and is riveting his attention to the sound of the gun and the toss of the dummy, you can increase the distance of the retrieve. Have the helper stay in the same place. You move the dog back to increase the distance. You do not want your dog to run over old retrieves. Start the marking drills on grass and move to heavy cover and different terrain, increasing the difficulty of the marked retrieves.

You can do the same type of marked drills in the water. Start out by having the helper throw the dummy from the side of the pond. Gradually have him move to the other side of the pond for longer retrieves. After several practice sessions, your dog will learn to use his eyes to watch the bird and mark where it falls. It is possible to have a pointing dog with a strong prey drive and strong desire become an outstanding natural retriever. Many versatile dogs make great retrieves over tough terrain and jump into icy moving water to chase down a crippled duck. It's a thrill to watch your dog consistently retrieve the birds you shoot. It is all a part of a complete versatile hunting dog.

Belle with a wood duck.

Tracking:
Dog Work After the Shot

Tracking, along with retrieving, is the work that your dog does after the shot and after the bird is killed or wounded. A track is the scent markings that a bird leaves when he walks or runs in the field. The bird's scent is left on the ground and in the air. A dog that is a good tracker has learned to pick up and identify this scent and follow it, whatever the distance, until he finds the dead or wounded bird.

Unfortunately, tracking is often the most neglected part of a pointing dog's training and can result in a disappointing hunt. For example, your dog has made a great point, you flush and shoot the bird, but when you and the dog get to where the bird fell, it isn't there, indicating that the bird is only wounded and is running. You begin to search the area but your dog, instead of looking for the wounded bird, is casting about in the field in search of more game. Because your dog hasn't been trained to track, you have to abandon the search and lose a beautiful bird. Hunters should make every effort to recover all shot birds. Recovery of birds is an ethical and important part of the hunt. A dog that is taught how to track will recover 90% or more of your wounded birds. Teaching a dog to track is both easy and fun, and a dog can be taught at any age to track.

Releasing the pheasant-note the feather left on the ground at the release site.

The pheasant runs into the field.

Versatile dog breeds were developed in Europe because hunters needed one dog that could hunt upland birds and waterfowl as well as track both birds and big game. This became necessary because almost all of the hunting in Europe is done on private land, and hunters are expected to recover all of the game they shoot. If a hunter fails to do so, he will not be invited to return for another hunt. Thus, a dog that can find downed game becomes an invaluable asset to a hunter. European dogs are taught to follow both a blood track and a scent track. When hunting big game in Europe, the dog sits by the hunter's stand or follows at heel if the hunter is stalking an animal. When the animal is shot, the dog is expected to track and find it. When the dog locates the animal, he stays by it and barks to let the hunter know where the animal has fallen. The same importance is placed on a dog's ability to track game birds. European tests held for the versatile breeds consist of both blood-tracking game animals and scent-tracking game birds.

Here in North America, the North American Versatile Hunting Dog Association (NAVHDA) has a tracking test for birds only. The JGV USA has both fur and feather tracking tests. Since most states prohibit hunting big game with a dog, there is little emphasis placed on tracking big game in the United States.

Teaching a young dog to track is fairly easy. Tracking can be taught in two ways: with a structured training format, or natural tracking that occurs out in the field with wild birds. It's helpful to have two or more people participate in a training session: one person to handle the dog and one to take care of the bird. Teaching a dog to track is an ideal way for two or more handlers to help each other in a joint training session. I like to use a pheasant for tracking because it is a big bird and gives off a great deal of scent. When setting a track, leave the dog in your rig. You don't want the dog to see where the bird runs. Tracking must be done by scent, not sight. Use a field that has ground cover at least ankle deep and also has some pockets of cover that are taller. Ideally, the bird should run out fifty yards or more and then hunker down and hide. Use duct tape to tape the pheasant's wings to its body, making sure that the wings are taped securely so that it can't fly away. Make sure the pheasant's legs are free so that it can run. After taping the wings, pull some of the smaller feathers from the breast area off the bird and place them on the ground where you intend to release the bird.

Next, with gloves on, take the pheasant in both hands and rub its breast on the ground in front of the feathers. It's important to have as much scent at the starting point as possible. Once you release the bird, it will usually run away from you. Clap your hands, whistle, or yell to encourage the bird to run and keep running. If the bird doesn't run, throw some small stones to scare it into running. Avoid walking out in the field to get the pheasant moving, because your scent will confuse the dog. I have found it is also helpful to leave a hat next to the starting point, behind the bird feathers, so that I can relocate it easily. It's amazing how quickly you can lose sight of the small pile of feathers in the cover.

When the pheasant has gone out to the desired distance and can no longer be seen, it's time to have the handler bring up his dog. Getting a dog started properly is very important. You want the dog to track the taped bird rather than search the field for new birds. Often a dog will charge from the starting point and cover the field hunting for birds. Take your lead off the dog and then pass it through and loop it around his collar. Hold on to both ends of the lead and then quietly and slowly, bring the dog up to

Bringing the dog up to the release point and turning him loose at the "Track" command.

where the pheasant was released. Pick a command that you intend to use when you want to tell your dog to track. I use the command *hunt dead*. When you reach the feathers left on the ground, stop the dog and make sure that he has time to get a good nose full of the scent. Give your dog the *hunt dead* command. You might have to push the dog's head gently into the feathers if he doesn't put his nose into them. When the dog has clearly smelled the bird, slowly let it start following the track. Keep the dog on the lead for ten or fifteen feet, helping him stay on the track. When the dog is tracking the bird, let go of one end of the lead and release him. Stand still and do not talk to the dog; let him do his job without distractions. Don't be surprised if your dog loses the track the first time. Often, a dog may overrun the track in his enthusiasm to get the bird. Remain calm. In many cases the dog will circle back and pick up the track. Give the dog plenty of time to locate and follow the track. While most dogs track with their head down, some dogs hold their heads high. This isn't important as long as the dog is deliberately tracking. If the dog loses the track and can't seem to pick it back up, call him back to you, take him by the collar and lead him to where he lost the track. Let him get a good scent and release him again. Often this restart is all you will need to get the dog back on the bird's track.

Most dogs pick up tracking very quickly; in many cases two or three sessions are all that is necessary to teach them. Remember that versatile dogs were bred in Europe to have a strong tracking instinct. Because the instinct and disposition is already in place, all you have to do is expose the dog to tracking and show it how you want it to track. Training sessions bring out the tracking instinct and build it into a strong quality.

If your dog is having problems catching on to tracking, there are ways to help him. One of the biggest problems dogs have is leaving the track and searching the field for birds. If this occurs, keep your dog on the lead for the entire track. Make sure that the person who released the bird knows the exact direction in which the bird ran so

Note pup with his head down tracking the pheasant.

that he can tell you where the track is. I like to draw a simple map on a piece of paper showing the direction the bird takes. By keeping your dog on a lead, he is forced to work slowly and to stay on the track and concentrate on his job. If your dog has trouble picking up the scent and following it, use a dead bird. Pull feathers out and leave them at the starting point. Attach a rope to the dead bird, drag it out fifty yards or more, and hide it. The body scent of the dragged bird, which is much stronger than the running feet of a live bird, should be strong enough to enable the dog to pick up and follow the scent. I recommend that the first few tracks should be done into the wind, giving a dog the extra advantage of tracking into the wind. Later in the training session, run the bird crosswind and downwind. You can't count on a wounded bird always running upwind.

One fall, we hunted pheasant in some of Montana's CRP fields in which the cover was exceptionally heavy, over six feet high in many places, and difficult to walk through. Blanche and our friends, Jim Tenuto and Chris Francis, were set up as blockers at the sides and ends of the field, while I took Duke and broke through the field. Duke stopped and pointed a number of times, only to have the birds run out on us. As we got to the middle of the field, pheasants started rocketing out at the ends and sides of the cover, providing the blockers with some great long-range shooting. At the end of the field, Duke locked up on point. As I took a step closer, a cackling rooster shot out in front of me. I shot immediately and hit the bird but didn't have time for a second shot because it fell down into thick cover. I knew that the bird had been hit too far back and wasn't dead. I released Duke, and he started through the cover in search of the running bird. Although I couldn't see Duke, I was able to hear him as he crashed through the field. The cover was as thick as a jungle, and I would never have been able to find a wounded bird in it by myself. But I had Duke and his nose in my favor, and after about five minutes and over two hundred yards later, I heard Duke stop. Moments later, I heard him coming back toward me. He had the wounded pheasant in his mouth, and both of his eyes were closed due to the briars he was running through. Without him, we would have lost that pheasant and many more that day.

Duke went to the veterinarian after that hunt to have his eyes flushed and get some medication to reduce the redness and irritation. I'm sure he would run through that heavy cover again in spite of what it did to his eyes. Jim wrote me the next week, thanking me for a great time. He closed the letter by saying, "Duke is the talk of southern California for his ability to handle pheasants and find wounded birds." That about says it all.

All of these methods work well in teaching your dog to track. You can use one or a combination of all of these methods. The important point is to teach your dog to track. You want all of your birds recovered. Tracking, along with retrieving, is the work the dog does after the shot. It is the completion of a successful hunt.

DK Bess Von Speidel, 4½-months-old. photo by Matt Oaks

A NAVHDA entourage during a Utility field test.

Advanced Training Methods:
Training Your Dog to Be a Brag Dog

The term "brag dog" is an old term that knowledgeable dog people use to describe the exceptional bird dog. "Jim really has a brag dog. He's a real bird finder; look at his intensity on point. He is rock solid, steady to wing, shot, and fall, and he whips out there, scoops up the dead bird and retrieves to hand."

All dog men wish for and hope to have a brag dog. It takes several elements to create such an animal. First the dog must have the natural ability inherited from his bloodlines. In the first part of our book we covered how to develop your dog's natural ability. Hopefully you spent the first year in bringing out all of his natural abilities: his use of nose, desire to hunt, and ability to search the field. Once your dog has had one year in the field hunting and has built his enthusiasm and developed his natural ability, you can start the advanced training. Now is the time to put the controls on your dog: to whoa train him; to make sure he is a totally dependable retriever; and to teach him to back. In the case of the versatile breeds, we also want to put the controls on the waterwork. We need a dog that is steady in the blind; that walks at heel while jump shooting ducks; and that can go out in the river or lake and hunt for and retrieve a wounded bird.

I will share with you the training techniques that the pros use to finish their bird dogs and build brag dogs. If you follow these training methods you should produce a dog that is head and shoulders above other pointing dogs. How will you know that you have successfully trained and finished your bird dog? The North American Versatile Hunting Dog Association (NAVHDA) has an advanced test, the Utility Test, which tests all of the qualities a versatile pointing dog should have to be considered a complete bird dog. Other versatile dog organizations have similar tests. As written in NAVHDA's test rules, "The utility test is designed to test a hunting dog's usefulness to the foot hunter in all phases of hunting, both before and after the shot, in field and marsh and on different species of game. The dog that successfully completes the Utility Test will

Jim Finner waits with his Pudelpointer for the start of the fieldwork in the Utility Test.

have demonstrated that he is a master, or at the very least a good solid hunter."

NAVHDA has chapters in all parts of the country and they run hundreds of tests each year. Their tests are open to all pointing dog breeds. There are setters and English pointers that run and are successful in passing the Utility Test. People are welcome to come and watch a test. I highly recommend that you at least go to a test and see what is required of a finished bird dog. You can successfully train your dog and end up with a brag dog without participating in a Utility Test. However, it provides the best standard I know of to evaluate your dog's progress and his success. The Utility Test requirements contain all of the attributes that a pointing dog must have to be considered a complete bird dog. Let's take a look at this challenging and demanding test.

The test is divided into two groups: fieldwork and waterwork. The dog's use of nose, desire to work, and cooperation with his handler, obedience, and stamina are judged throughout the test. Each of these elements is judged in every aspect of the test. Every NAVHDA test has three judges who evaluate and score the dog.

The fieldwork is done in a bird field over varied terrain containing several game birds. The handler carries an unloaded gun and there are two gunners whose job is to shoot the birds. The duration of the fieldwork is thirty minutes. The handler and his dog are to go out and engage in a productive search. When the dog finds a bird he is judged on his pointing ability. Steadiness is also required. A dog must be steady to wing, shot, and fall in order to pass. The judges look for confident, quiet sportsmen-like teamwork between the handler and his dog. Any commands given to whoa the dog will cause a reduction in score. After the bird is shot the hunter can then give a command for his dog to retrieve. The retrieve should be quick and eager with the bird being delivered to hand.

The second part of the fieldwork is the retrieval of dead game. This part of the test judges a dog's ability and willingness to retrieve game on its own without the influence of its handler. One of the judges will drag a dead bird between one hundred and two hundred yards so that the bird is out of sight of the handler. He will then leave the bird and proceed on for a short distance where he will hide. His job is to watch what the dog does. This is important since some dogs, when they are out of sight of their handlers, will abandon the search or mishandle or bury the bird. After the bird is placed, the other judges call up the handler and his dog. The handler then releases his dog with one command, telling him to go fetch. The dog should run out, pick up the bird without hesitation and quickly bring it back to the handler and deliver it to hand. This demonstrates the dog's cooperation and obedience.

Relentless pursuit of a duck in the search for the duck part of the test.

Since we are training a versatile dog, waterwork is as important as the dog's ability in the field. The reason we have a versatile dog is so we can hunt geese in the morning, upland birds midday, and finish off with a late afternoon duck hunt; all with the same dog, who can do it all and do it well.

The search for the duck is a test of the dog's ability to locate and retrieve wounded waterfowl on its own, without the handler helping the dog or giving it commands. There are many situations where a wounded duck falls into a pond and swims into the cattails or hides where the hunter cannot see it or know for sure where it is. We want our dogs to rely on their own initiative and bird-finding ability to go out into the water and search for and find the wounded or dead bird. This is a test that judges the dog's nose, desire, perseverance, and stamina. A pond of at least one acre, preferably more, is used. The pond should have sufficient vegetation for the duck to swim to and hide. The water must have some areas that are at swimming depth for the dog. The judges clip the feathers of one wing of a duck so it cannot fly. They then toss the duck into the water. The duck will naturally swim away from the judges and hide itself in the vegetation. During this time the handler and the dog are out of sight and cannot hear or see where the duck goes. After the duck has hidden itself, the handler and his dog are called up to the bank. The handler is given a shotgun and a blank load. The handler sets his dog up on the bank. The dog should remain quietly still until given the command to search and retrieve the duck. The handler fires a blank in the air and is allowed to give his dog one command only. The successful dog will go into the water and systematically search the water and cover in and around the pond. Each dog is allowed at least ten minutes to search out the duck. The dog is judged on the thoroughness of his search, his desire, use of nose, stamina, intelligence and perseverance. The dog does not have to find the duck to pass the test. However, if the dog finds the duck and catches it, then he must successfully retrieve the duck to the handler. A dog that will go out and search relentlessly for a duck that he did not see fall without repeated handling and commands from his handler is a superior dog.

The next part of the waterwork deals with how the dog handles walking at heel, remaining steady in a blind, and retrieving a bird in the water while swimming through decoys. A small pond is used and a blind is set up on the bank. A person with a dead duck is located on the land across the pond. The hunter is asked to walk his dog at heel on a loose lead through a zigzag course near the pond. Stakes are used and are set about thirty-six inches apart. The handler and his dog must walk through the stakes. The dog should do so at heel without any harsh commands, or pulling on the lead. This is a basic test of the dog's obedience. Right after this part of the test the handler must place his dog, with the lead off, either in the blind or at one side of the blind. The handler is given a shotgun and two blank shells. He is allowed to give his dog a command to stay. The handler is instructed to walk to a hidden spot where his dog cannot see him. He then fires the blanks with a delay of at least ten seconds between the two shots. He then returns to the blind. The dog must remain calmly and quietly by the blind, awaiting the return of his handler. A dog that leaves the blind completely does not pass that part of the test. The final part of this test judges the dog's ability to remain calm in the presence of repeated gunfire. This replicates the actual situation in a duck blind where the ducks come in and there are repeated shots taken by the hunters. You want a dog that will not be jumping out of the blind until given the command to retrieve. The handler positions his dog in the blind or to one side. The dog can be lying down, sitting, or standing. There is a second gunner placed out of sight of the blind. Both the handler and the gunner are given blanks. On a signal from one of the judges, the gunner fires one blank, followed by the handler firing one blank, and then the gunner fires another blank. Now, the person located on the other side of the pond throws the duck into the air and out into the water. The duck is thrown so the dog can easily see it. When the duck is in the air, the handler fires the final blank. When the duck hits the water, the handler gives his dog the command to fetch the duck. The dog should then enter the water, swim through the decoys, pick up the duck and swim back to the bank, retrieving the duck to the handler. During the firing sequence the dog is required to remain steady and calm by the blind. When retrieving the duck, the dog can shake upon emerging from the water but will be penalized if he drops the duck. At any time during the retrieving of birds by the dog in either the water or field part of the test, if the dog willfully mutilates any bird as to render it unfit for the table, it cannot receive a passing score.

In most cases, owners train their own dogs to run in and pass the Utility Test. It is a truly tough test that sets very high-performance standards for both the dog and his handler. The dog that can successfully handle all of the hunting situations that occur in both field and water and pass the NAVHDA Utility Test deserves the accolade of brag dog.

A blank is fired prior to the dog being sent in a water retrieve.

*Chris Hall's Red Setter Ryland. The first Red Setter
to obtain a Prize I in a NAVHDA Utility Test.
photos by Chris Hall*

Getting together with friends is a great way to not only have help in training while you handle your dog-but you also might be able to share costs and equipment.

Advanced Training - The Essentials:
Time, Land, Equipment, and Temperament

One of the most satisfying experiences for a bird hunter is training a young pointing dog. Since you and your dog will spend many days in the field hunting together, your dog will become your favorite hunting partner. Training your own dog helps develop a close bond, which makes the two of you a great hunting team. I highly recommend that you personally work with your dog during his first year. Most trainers do not have the time to take a young pup out into the bird field and hunt him on wild birds. Your dog has bonded with you and wants to please you. You can do a much better job of developing your dog's natural abilities than a trainer. It is a great deal of fun and you will find a special satisfaction in watching your young hunting dog develop during his first year.

Putting the controls on a dog takes a lot of knowledge and equipment. You might want to have a trainer finish your dog and force break him and whoa train him. Before you decide whether to use a professional trainer for this advanced training, let's go over what it will take for you to do it yourself so that you can make an informed decision about this critical time in your young dog's training.

Advanced dog training requires a great deal of time and some expense on the your part. When your dog was young and you were exposing him to the field and birds, letting him develop his natural ability, your dog had very little pressure put on him. During the second phase of developing and finishing a bird dog, you will be putting restraints on him. You will be encountering some resistance on his part. It will also take a great deal of time, persistence, and patience to complete the advanced training.

Before we start, let's go over the essential elements that you need to ensure that your training will be successful. It takes time to train a bird dog. If you want your dog to be completely whoa trained, and be a reliable retriever, on both land and water, then you can expect to take between four and six months to complete the various training sessions. The ideal situation is to train three times a week. It is best to give both you and your dog a day off between training sessions. The only exception to this is when you are working on the trained retrieve. Then the training consists of ten-minute sessions twice daily. A good schedule for the rest of your training would be Monday-Wednesday-Friday, or Tuesday-Thursday-Sunday. While each training session will be between twenty to forty minutes, you have to add your travel time. Unless you live in the country where you have the land on which to train, you will need to drive to a training area. While my house is on eight acres, most of my advanced training is at a state land area that is a thirty-minute drive from my house. So let's figure an average of two hours per training session three times a week. That means a commitment of six hours a week. Many of the training sessions will require you to shoot birds. You will need a training area that allows you to train dogs and fire a gun. Most states require a license or permit for bird dog training. In Montana we have to fill out a form stating the area on which we intend to train and we also must list the birds that we intend to use. Our fish and game department must sign and approve the application. Game bird breeders are not allowed to sell game birds to people who do not have either a preserve license or a training license. If you have a versatile dog, you will also need a training area that has a pond for your water training. It is best to have at least two different areas in which to train. I have seen situations where a dog that is trained at only one place will perform flawlessly at that one place. However, when you take the dog to a different area when you go hunting, he does not perform well. You will be hunting your dog in a number of different places. It makes sense to train him in different places so he understands that he must perform the same, no matter where he is hunting.

Putting the controls on your dog can be a frustrating time for both you and your dog. It takes a great deal of patience to successfully train a dog. Whoa training, teaching steadiness by the blind, and retrieving training take a great deal of time. Success is measured in very small increments. You can go through the same drill for a week or two and sometimes see very little progress. Right now, I am training a young dog to force break to retrieve. We have had two training sessions a day for the past eight days. The dog is still resisting opening her mouth to accept the training dummy. You must be prepared to accept bumps in the training process. Each dog is different. Some dogs progress and catch on quickly; others take more time. Patience is very important and is one of the necessary keys for a trainer to be successful. If you try to rush the process and skip steps, you will likely create problems and not be completely successful in finishing your bird dog.

Your temperament is the other essential key to success in training. If you get frustrated and lose your temper, you will set back your dog's training and create a number of problems for your dog. Remember, you will be putting a lot of pressure on your dog. He will be exposed to situations that are new and frightening to him. If he also sees you lose your temper and start shouting at him, he will most likely shut down and refuse to cooperate. It is important to be calm and encourage your dog at all times during the training pro- cess. Every time he does some-

It takes a lot of birds to train a bird dog. It is best to have your own bird pen.

thing right, praise him with a soft voice. Make sure he understands that you are really happy that he is doing it right. Sage, the young dog that I am force breaking, is doing one thing right. Once I get the dummy in her mouth, she holds it until I give her the command to give it to me. I must put pressure on her with an ear pinch to get her to open her mouth. She resists this. However, once she is holding the dummy I praise her and tell her in a soft voice what a good dog she is. I also stroke her side gently, showing her how pleased I am with that part of her training.

It is also important for you to be able to read your dog. A good trainer knows what a dog is going to do and how it is going to react by reading its body language and expressions. Dog training is a combination of art and science. Every dog responds dif- ferently to training and a trainer who understands dogs will modify his techniques to fit the dog's personality.

Training your own bird dog can be very rewarding. However, you have to decide if you have the time and the temperament to do it yourself and to be successful. You will need a lot of birds and a great deal of equipment for your dog training. Remem- ber, it takes birds to make a bird dog. A dog that is whoa trained is one who points and holds his point; is steady, allowing the hunter to flush and shoot the bird; and waits for the hunter to give him a command to retrieve before he moves. In order to whoa train you will need birds, preferably pigeons that can be planted and flushed while you teach your dog steadiness. In the finishing stages of whoa training you will be killing birds for your dog. You can use pigeons for this stage. However, during the final sessions I recommend using either quail or chukars. You will need at least thirty to forty pigeons and twenty to thirty game birds. You will also need bird feed, a bird crate to carry the birds, and a pigeon and quail pen to house the birds. For the water training you will need six to eight ducks. You will also need at least four pheasants for retriever training.

APPROXIMATE COST FOR BIRDS — DEPENDING ON YOUR AREA:

- Pigeons - 30 at $3.00 each: $90.00
- Quail - 30 at $6.00 each: $180.00
- Ducks - 6 at $10.00 each: $60.00
- Pheasants – 4 at $15.00 each: $60.00
- Bird carrying pen: $55.00
- Quail pen construction: $200.00
- Pigeon pen construction: $200.00
- Duck pen construction: $150.00
    Total $995.00

APPROXIMATE COST OF THE TRAINING EQUIPMENT:

- Training pistol and holster: $60.00
- Blanks for training pistol (1 box of 100): $8.00
- Popper loads for shotgun - 2 boxes of 25 at $10.00 each: $20.00
- Shotgun shells - 2 boxes at $5.00 each: $10.00
- Dog lead: $10.00
- Check cord: $10.00
- Pinch collar: $24.00
- Electric collar: $250.00
- Automatic release bird traps – 2 at $230 each: $460.00
- 6 duck decoys: $25.00
- 6 canvas dummies at $4.00 each: $24.00
- Retriever launcher: $65.00
- Dog silhouette for backing - self made: $10.00
    Total: $976.00

Your total costs in equipment and birds will be around $2,000.

It takes quite an investment in birds and equipment to train a bird dog. I recommend that you get together and train with several other people. You can form a group of your hunting buddies or you can check to see if you have a local bird dog club that you can join that has training grounds and members with whom you can train. Some of the advanced training takes several people. In the final stages of whoa training, it is best to have two gunners in addition to the dog handler. The training sessions are easier and more fun with a small group rather than doing it on your own. Another big advantage of group training is that you can share some of the equipment expenses with the group, such as the costs for the bird pens, decoys, and bird launchers.

Now that you have an idea of the time involved and the expense, you have to decide whether or not you want to do the advanced training yourself or let a professional trainer do it for you. Training your own dog is a rewarding experience and will give you a great deal of satisfaction and pride when the job is done. There is no greater thrill then having your hunting buddies look in awe as your dog pins down a running pheasant, points it, holds the bird there until you are able to flush and kill it, and then makes a retrieve to hand. You know then you have a brag dog.

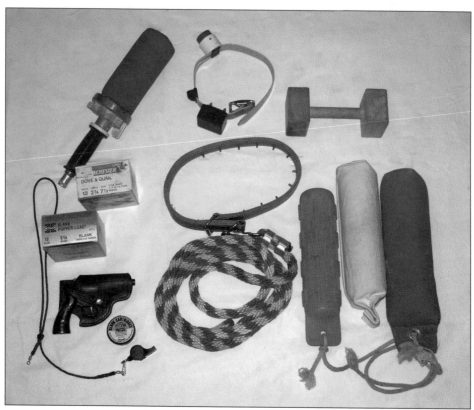

Here is the essential equipment you'll need for training.

DK Kurzhaar on point.

John Kegel, one of the founders of NAVHDA, and his wife with one of our puppies.

Using a Professional Trainer

Let's assume that you have decided to have your dog trained by a professional trainer. You have heard your friends mention several names of trainers and there are a number of ads in *The Pointing Dog Journal* and other bird dog magazines. How do you decide which trainer to use? There are some key questions that you can ask to ensure that you are picking the right person to train your dog.

Q: *What type of dogs does the trainer normally train?*
If you own a versatile breed and want to run your dog in a NAVHDA Utility Test, for example, it would make sense to use a trainer who trains versatile breeds for both hunting and NAVHDA tests. If you live in Wisconsin and hunt grouse and woodcock, you would be better served with a trainer who lives in a major grouse state and specializes in training close-working grouse dogs. On the other hand, if you spend most of your time hunting the wide prairies of the west, you want to pick a trainer from that area who has access to that type of terrain.

 Many people make the mistake of picking a trainer who has a great reputation in training and winning horseback field trials. A field trial trainer's program is geared to big-running dogs. He makes his living by running in and winning on the field trial circuit. The vast majority of hunters want a dog they can hunt with on foot. Look for a trainer who handles hunting dogs, not just field trial dogs.

Q: How many dogs does the trainer have in his kennel at any one time?
Most trainers take no more than twelve to fourteen dogs at a time. If a trainer has too many dogs to train, he will not be able to devote the time necessary to train them properly. This number can vary depending on the type of training being done. If you are whoa training older dogs, you will be spending more time with each dog. If you are training a lot of puppies that take fifteen- to twenty-minute sessions twice a day, you can train more dogs.

Q: What type of training areas does the trainer use?
Basic commands can be taught in a small yard area. However, a trainer should also have available a large area similar to the type of terrain in which the dog will be hunting wild birds. If you want your dog trained for waterwork, a pond is essential.

Q: What type of facilities does the trainer have and what type of dog food does he feed?
You are going to be leaving your dog with the trainer for three or four months. Make sure that he has a clean, safe kennel. A good trainer will have a kennel facility that has individual kennels and kennel runs for each dog. Ask what kind of dog food your dog will be fed. I once made the mistake of leaving my dogs for four weeks with a highly recommended kennel for boarding while we were in the process of moving from Ohio to Montana. When I came to pick up my dogs, I found that they had lost over 30% of their body weight and had open sores on their bodies. The kennel owner had run out of dog food and was also short of money. My vet told me that in her opinion, the dogs had not been fed for more than two weeks. Fortunately, my vet was able to save my dogs.

Q: What references can he give you?
Ideally, you should get the names of three or four people who have recently had their dogs trained by the trainer you are considering. Call these dog owners and ask them if they were satisfied with the results. Did their dogs receive the quality of care that they expected? What problems, if any, did they encounter?

Q: Can you visit the trainer and spend some time with him while he trains dogs?
Most trainers are willing to let you visit their facilities and observe a training session. While he is training dogs, watch the dogs' reactions to the trainer. Do they like him? Do they respond eagerly to his commands? If you see dogs in training that have their tails down and show fear of the trainer, beware! While you are visiting, you'll get the chance to check out the kennels. Are they clean? Do all the dogs appear well fed and healthy?

So, you've done your homework; you've checked out a number of trainers and decided on one to train your dog. Now it's time to discuss with the trainer exactly what you want accomplished. Describe your normal hunting day, the type of birds you hunt, and how hard you hunt. Be realistic in your expectations. Many dog owners ask for their dogs to be steady to wing and shot. A dog that stands totally steady to wing, shot, and fall is a beautiful sight, but it is also very difficult to maintain that level of training. You will need to spend a great deal of time, both in the field and in yard work, to keep your dog steady. Realistically, very few hunters have the expertise or patience to maintain that level of training.

Your trainer will need a month to bond with your dog and gain his confidence. You can't rush a training program and expect good results, so your dog will be in training for three or four months, perhaps longer. At this writing, most hunting dog trainers charge from $450 to $650 per month. When the trainer starts shooting pen-raised birds over your dog, you will be expected to pay extra for the birds.

Be involved in the training process. You will be handling your dog in the field after he is trained and will need to know what commands to use and how he was trained. It's a waste of your money and the trainer's time and effort if you do not understand the training process. Your dog needs to know that you are involved in his training, and that he will be hunting with you, not the trainer, in the field during the hunting season.

Most failures in dog training are not the dog's fault, but the lack of understanding and follow-through by the owner. Plan to spend time with the trainer when you pick your dog up at the end of the training program. Have your trainer go over all of the commands and methods used in training. Ask your trainer what you can do to maintain this peak level of performance. After you bring your dog home, you will have an adjustment period in which you will have to re-establish your bond with your dog. Your pup bonded with the trainer; now he needs some time to bond back with you.

Hunting with your bird dog is like dancing; it's not about controlling and handling the dog. The hunter and his dog should be a like a dance team, working seamlessly together to produce birds. Learn to ease up on control and let your dog make mistakes and learn how to work the birds. He will be a better hunting dog for you if you learn to trust him. He will learn how to handle, point, and hold birds for you. Go out and have a good time with your canine partner - that's what hunting is all about.

John Shewey's Weimaraner, Asa's Outlaw Josie Wiles. photo by John Shewey

Proper Use of the E-collar for Training and Communication with Your Dog

The electronic collar, or e-collar, is an excellent tool in the advanced training process. While you can whoa train a dog without the e-collar, it will make your job easier. The e-collar is also an excellent tool for reinforcing whoa in the bird field and allows you to communicate with your dog while hunting. I go into detail as to how to use the collar for communication in the chapter, *How to Handle Your Dog in the Field*. Most people misuse the collar. They regard it as a means to punish the dog. They also use it when the dog does not know what he is supposed to be doing. Overuse of the e-collar at an early age can ruin a young dog.

All collars work on the basis of electrical stimulation. The collar has a box on it that has two prongs that transmit the stimulation. The collar fits snugly around the dog's neck. There is a transmitter that you hold in order to control the stimulation. The best collars have many advanced features that are essential in doing the job without hurting your dog.

There are many types and makes of collars on the market today. Here are the essential elements that your collar should have in order to work for you:

- **Momentary Stimulation:** You press a button and the collar gives a quick second of stimulation and then the stimulation stops. In most of your training cases you will only need momentary stimulation

- **Continuous Stimulation:** You press a button on the transmitter and the stimulation continues until you take your finger off the button. This feature should rarely be used.

- **Variable Levels of Stimulation:** You want a collar that has a number of stimulation levels from the very lowest, where there is no pain only a vibration, up to a hot button to be used only in extreme circumstances. Most collars have ten or more levels.

- **Tone-Only:** This is one of the most important features on a collar. You should be able to set your collar to emit a tone only. This is a great way to communicate with your dog. You can tell him, "OK, I know you are on point. Hold your point until I get there." You can start your control training with a tone followed by a momentary stimulation on a low level. Your dog will soon associate the tone with the command. He will also learn that if he does not obey the command it will be followed with stimulation. Once your dog is trained, the tone-only feature reminds him of what he is trained to do.

- **Collar Range:** Most collars have a range of one quarter of a mile. If you are hunting big country a range of one half mile is even better.

- **Beeper Feature:** Many hunters use a bell or a beeper collar on their dog. It enables them to know where their dog is hunting. The best e-collars have a built-in beeper feature. I like the collar that allows me to use the beeper in silent mode. I prefer this to a collar that is constantly beeping. I can set the collar to beep when the dog has stopped for seven seconds or more. When I hear the collar I know the dog is on point. Also I can turn the beeper on if I want to locate my dog. Finally, by holding a button down the beeper will continue to beep. I use this feature to call my dog back to me. My dogs have learned that more than one beep means, "Check back with me".

- **Multiple Features:** I prefer collars that will let me handle two dogs at a time and will also let me work automatic bird launchers from them.

I have seen a number of dogs ruined for hunting by misuse or overuse of the e-collar. The biggest temptation for a new puppy owner is to put a collar on his pup. Instead of letting the young puppy run and have fun, building up his desire and search, the owner continues to shock the dog in order to keep him by his side. Soon the dog learns that he will get hurt if he ventures out too far, so he stays right at his owner's side. The owner has made him a boot licker. Never use the e-collar on a dog before one year of age and before he has had one hunting season. I get more phone calls and e-mails about the problem of overusing the collar on a young dog than any other training problem. The problem is always a variation of the situation I described above. The owner now wants to know how to undo the problem. He has a dog with a low tail and one that is afraid to hunt. In many cases the dog has started to blink his birds. Blinking birds is a situation in which a dog knows where the bird is, but he deliberately avoids pointing it. He will often leave it. Dogs do this because, in most cases, they have been hit too many times with an e-collar.

FOLLOW THESE BASIC RULES WHEN USING YOUR COLLAR:

- Use the collar to correct a dog's actions only when you know the dog already clearly understands and knows what he is supposed to be doing. He must know the command you are trying to enforce.
- Use the collar only if you can make a correction within two seconds or less. Your dog must relate the stimulation to his mistake.
- Use the lowest stimulation possible. Each dog is different. Most dogs are sensitive enough that you can use a very low level of stimulation in training; the lower the better.
- The e-collar is not a tool to punish a dog.

The only time that you should use high stimulation is in a situation where your dog is going to be in danger: running out into the street into traffic or running onto the railroad tracks when a train is coming.

It is important to properly fit the collar on your dog. The collar should be snug so that the prongs make contact with the skin. However, if you get the collar too tight you can cut off the dog's ability to breath. The closer you place the collar to your dogs' head the more severe the stimulation will be. Start with the collar behind his regular collar.

When you start to use the e-collar, it is extremely important that you determine which level of stimulation to use on your dog. All dogs have a different threshold for pain. Start with the lowest stimulation and watch your dog's reaction. Look closely at his ears, head, and eyes. Any movement no matter how slight, a turn of the head, a small movement of the ear or tail, means the dog is feeling the stimulation. This is the level you want to use. When you make a correction with the collar and your dog obeys, make sure that you praise him. You want him to know when he is doing the right thing. It is very important that your dog understands when he is doing what you want him to do. Lavish praise will help speed up your dog's training and minimize the use of the e-collar.

It is important to introduce the e-collar to your dog in a positive way. You want him to associate the collar with the things he wants to do most; the activities he loves. I start all of my dogs hunting wild birds the fall of their first year. In most cases they are only fourteen to sixteen weeks old. After their first four or five hunts, and when their neck is big enough for the e-collar to fit, I put the collar on them when I take them out of the rig and run them in the bird field. I do not turn the collar on. I want them to get used to wearing the collar and associate it with the hunting experience. Soon my puppy is excited to get the collar put on him. He knows that means he is going hunting; the activity he loves more than anything else in his life. I do not usually use the e-collar during the pup's first season. However, I want him to connect the fact that the e-collar means bird hunting. When I start training him in his second year with the collar, it is much easier and faster because my young dog already has a positive feeling about the collar.

There is only one time that I will use the e-collar on a young dog, and that is to teach him to come when called. However, I will not use the collar even for that command until he has worn it for five or six times and is excited to have me put it on him. I cover the use of the e-collar to enforce the *come* command in the section on Camas.

The Trained Retrieve:
Phase One

Recently, my friend John Crozier, a NAVHDA senior judge and clinic leader, came to Boise, Idaho to run a handler's clinic. One of the great things about NAVHDA is the sharing of information. In the evening, John explained to me his method of training his dogs to retrieve. He calls it the trained retrieve instead of forced retrieve. I thought his method was excellent. John is a breeder of German wirehaired pointers and also trains pointing dogs.

The trained retrieve consists of three parts: Phase One, have the dog hold an object; Phase Two, have him reach and grasp the object; and Phase Three, have him travel to pick up and return the object to the handler. There are many steps in each part of the training, and one step builds on the other. Each step becomes the control for the next step, and must be mastered before moving on to the next step. If at any time the dog resists or becomes confused, go back to the last step the dog has mastered. Should a problem arise, it is very easy to fix the problem by reviewing the dog's performance; determining what the dog is not doing right and then going back to that step and working on it again until he masters it.

Once you have started the training process, do not stop until the dog is finished. One or two short ten-minute lessons a day is best. Do not start your lessons if you are tired or angry. Dogs can read humans very well, sensing the human's disposition and reacting to it. The trained retrieve is a very confusing and stressful training procedure for a dog. You do not want to make it more difficult by a negative attitude. Do not use the *fetch* command or your training dummy for anything other than the trained retrieve lessons. It will confuse the dog and set back your training.

Dogs like to please. Make sure that you give your dog praise when he does each step successfully. Smile, be animated, and let your body language show that you are pleased.

The left hand clears the lips from the teeth and is opening the mouth. The thumb on the right hand pulls the dummy against the lower canine teeth, and the finger support supports the jaw. Note the short lead wrapped around the left hand.
photo by John Crozier

The proper way to hold the dummy: thumb over the dummy, fingers which will go underneath the dog's mouth.
photo by John Crozier

YOU WILL NEED THE FOLLOWING EQUIPMENT:

- Twenty-five- to fifty-foot check cord
- Six-foot leash
- Dumb-bell type dummy
- Chain collar
- Eight- to ten-inch snap lead
- Training table – or raised platform
- Several weighted dummies, padded by duct tape: two-pound, four-pound, eight-pound, and ten-pound

The first step in Phase One is to get the dog to hold an object, a training dummy. By hold, John means a good firm grip. Do not accept a loose grip. If you do, then that is what you will have when the dog is a finished retriever.

Snap the eight-inch snap lead onto both rings of the chain collar so that the collar is not in a choke mode. We are not using the collar as a choke collar. Slip the collar over the dog's head. Position it right behind the base of his head. Maintaining this position is very important. The pressure points located just behind the dog's ears will be stimulated each time you snap the lead straight up over his head. This pressure will cause the dog to bite down on the dummy. Grasp the dummy with your right hand, palm up and open. Hook your thumb over the narrow part of the dummy. Your left hand is holding the snap lead above the dog's head. Now reach over the dog's head with the left hand, grasp the muzzle from above, clear the lips from the teeth, and lift open the mouth. If your dog will not open his mouth, use the thumb of your left hand to pinch the lip against the teeth. As you open the mouth, say *Fetch* and use your right hand to insert the dummy. Your thumb is hooked onto the dummy and your fingers go under the lower jaw. Place the dummy right behind the lower canines and then pull it up snug against the lower teeth with your thumb. As soon as the dummy is in place, give the *fetch* command again and snap the lead straight up and then give slack on the lead. This is a short snap that gets the dog's attention. It is not meant to lift him off the table, as if hanging him. Continue short snaps on the lead saying *Fetch* each time until you feel pressure on your thumb, which is still in the dog's mouth. When your dog has firmly grasped the dummy, give him praise. Now give him your release command and let him spit out or drop the dummy. At this stage we are not looking for the dog to hold the dummy for any length of time. Remember the longer you have the dog hold the dummy at this beginning stage the greater the chance he will relax his grip. Our goal is to get the dog to open his mouth, grasp firmly and take hold of the dummy when given a *fetch* command.

This first step is very important. It is not an easy step for the dog. He doesn't have a clue as to why you are snapping the chain and holding a dummy against his lower jaw. In the beginning your dog will most likely try to spit out the dummy. He will turn his head or use any other technique he can come up with to avoid it. Just persevere. Praise only when your dog takes the object and has a firm grip on it. Time your praise and give it the instant the dog takes a firm grip, not when he opens his mouth. Try to get the dog to do six to eight correct repetitions before you end each session. When your dog is consistently biting down and holding the dummy firmly for a few seconds when you give the *fetch* command and snap the lead it is time to move on to the next stage.

In the next stage of Phase One, you can remove your thumb from the dog's mouth. Grasp the dummy with the right hand and open the dog's mouth. Say *Fetch* and insert the dummy. At the same time snap up on the lead. Place your right hand under the dog's jaw. The right hand gives support and pressure, encouraging the dog to hold the dummy firmly. Test the dog's grip by putting the fingers of your right hand under his jaw. By feeling the jaw, you can tell whether or not he has a firm grip. Your dog should not try to spit the dummy out. When the dog is gripping the object, stop snapping, praise him and then give him the release command. Make sure that you do not give any praise as the dog relaxes his grip to release the dummy. If you do, you will be reinforcing the wrong behavior – i.e. relaxing his grip.

When your dog is grasping the dummy firmly for several sessions it is time to move on to the next stage of Phase One. In this stage we remove the right hand from under the dog's jaw. Open his mouth, insert the dummy saying *Fetch* and snap the lead. Do not put your right hand under the dog's mouth. Now you are going to alternate your right hand on and off the dog's lower jaw every few seconds. Each time you put your hand on or off the jaw say *Fetch* and snap the lead. Do not attempt to prolong the duration at this stage. It should be *fetch*, snap, *fetch*, snap, with a *Good Boy* command when your dog grasps the dummy firmly and then releases. As the sessions progress, start to alternate the process. Give the dog a *fetch* command, without the snap. We want to start eliminating the snap and the hand on the jaw as the dog learns to grasp the dummy with the *fetch* command.

When your dog maintains a constant grip throughout and performs six to eight perfect reps, it is time to completely eliminate the snap. Do the same routine without the snaps. If at any time the dog loosens his grip, give one quick snap. Your dog will respond by tightening his grip.

Now it's time to change your grip on the dummy. Hold the dummy by the end. With your right hand open the dog's mouth, keep the chain and lead on the dog, say *Fetch*, put the dummy in his mouth and remove your hand. We are gradually taking away the pressure points, your hand under the jaw and the snap, as the dog begins to understand what you want him to do and he consistently holds the dummy with a firm grip. Remember to keep your left hand in place with the chain and the lead so you can be ready to enforce the firm grip with a snap if necessary.

Once your dog is opening his mouth, letting you insert the dummy and holding it with a firm grip, it is time to move on to walking the dog at heel with the dummy in his mouth. Place your dog on the training table; put a chain collar on the dog well up on the neck; snap an eight- to ten-inch lead to both of the rings on the collar and have several barbell dummies ready.

This will be the first time that you have had to issue two commands that the dog must obey at the same time. Some dogs have a very hard time with this. You say *Fetch* and they hold the dummy, you say *Heel* and they drop the dummy or won't move. It

photos by John Crozier

The chain should be behind the ears - great pressure points.

Once a firm grip is achieved, the handler grasps the end of the dummy as pressure points are gradually diminished.

takes a little patience, but they will catch on. Start the dog on heel at the far end of the table. Do not go up or down the ramps as yet. You may need to say *Fetch, Heel, Fetch, Heel*, to get the dog walking without dropping the dummy. Keep an eye on the dog. Usually when he lowers his head he is thinking about dropping the dummy. When he can walk from one end of the table to the other without easing up on the grip or dropping the dummy, you are well on your way. Now start the dog at the bottom of the ramp and heel across the table. The next big step is to heel down the opposite side. For some reason or other, as soon as the dog hits the down ramp, his head will drop and so does the dummy. Knowing this, it is a good idea to anticipate that the dog will make a mistake and, just as you start down the ramp, give a quick *fetch*/snap reminder. It won't be long before the dog is heeling up and down and all around the table while continuing to hold the dummy. Now we can start to increase the duration of the grip. Go slowly at first and work up to a minute or more. Fill the duration with lavish praise. Why? Because the dog must learn that praise is not a release command and that he may not drop the dummy just because you are telling him he is a good boy. You are also praising the dog for doing a good job. You will see a change in the dog's demeanor while you do this. He will pep up, wag his tail and gain confidence. He knows the boss is happy. Now that the dog is heeling with the dummy and holding it for some time, you can gradually start doing things to get the dog to drop the dummy. This is done so you have an opportunity to correct the dog and he will quickly learn the dummy doesn't come out of his mouth until you give the release command.

With the dog on the table, open his mouth, give the *fetch* command and insert the dummy. Check the grip to be sure it's okay. Tap the ends of the dummy. The idea is to get the dog to loosen the grip. If he does, command *Fetch* and give the leash snap correction. Gradually work up to where you can grab the dummy and push down or pull up and the dog's head will follow. Also try to grab the dummy as if you were about to give the release command, just don't give the command. If the dog gives you the dummy, scold him. Say *Fetch*, putting the dummy back in his mouth and snap the lead/chain. In this way he will learn not to anticipate the release command just because you are reaching for the dummy. Now start to heel the dog and, while he is heeling, bump the dummy with your knee. I usually give a *fetch* command reminder just before bumping the dummy. If the dog drops the dummy, scold him *No!* Pick it up, say *Fetch* and put it in his mouth, giving the leash/chain correction.

Once the dog will tolerate this tempting and will not make any mistakes you can now start to have him hold and heel with objects of different texture e.g., rolled up magazine, water bottle half full of water so it sloshes, soda cans, hair brushes, keys, etc. Use your imagination. When introducing a different object, always start on the table. Check the grip, tempt him to drop it and when he does all this without a flaw, heel him around for several minutes. There is one last test to make sure that the dog's grip is steady and firm before moving on to Phase Two of his training: The Reach and Grasp Phase. Put on a thin leather glove and open the dog's mouth, say *Fetch* and insert your hand. You should feel a steady firm grip. If you don't, say *Fetch* and snap the lead. Most dogs do not want to apply pressure to your hand so it may take a few *fetch*/snaps for him to get the idea. When he grips with a steady and firm grip, give him a *heel* command with your hand still in his mouth. Most dogs will look at you with a "You've got to be kidding" look. Some won't move. Be patient and work through it; he will figure it out and, if you have made sure that each step has been mastered before you moved on to the next step, the dog will pass this final test with flying colors.

The dog must grasp your hand and "heel" before moving onto the reach and grasp phase.

The Trained Retrieve:
Phases Two and Three

The second phase in the trained retrieve is the reach-and-grasp phase. This phase is why many people choose not to do the trained retrieve, as it is the dreaded ear-pinch phase. In looking at the entire trained retrieve process, the ear pinch is only one small step. Once the dog reaches for and grasps the dummy, the ear pinch is done. But it can be a very trying time for the dog and a very emotional time for the handler. One word about the ear pinch: Some people grasp the end of the ear and pinch; some dogs will yelp (the response you want) but most will not. John goes to the entrance to the ear canal. He puts this portion of the ear against the buckle of the collar or against the nametag on the collar of the dog's regular flat collar. John thinks it is far more humane to make the pinch really hurt for a time or two, rather than make the dog whine and not yelp by not pinching hard enough. Also, a pinch that really hurts is not soon forgotten. You will find that as you move on, you can just grasp the ear and the dog will yelp without a pinch. You might want to do a dry-run ear pinch without a *fetch* command to make sure you can make the dog yelp. Some dogs are real stoics.

Now, put your left hand through the dog's flat collar and flip the ear over on the nameplate or buckle. With your right hand holding the dummy under the dog's jaw (to help control the dog's head), move the dummy out in front of the dog's mouth, about six inches away and level with the dog's eyes. It is very important to be aware of what your right hand is doing. It must *never* bring the dummy to the dog. You will find it helpful to actually lock your right elbow against your right hip joint; you are less apt to move the dummy to the dog this way. Now say, *Fetch* and start pinching the ear. The dog will yelp and start to bite or grasp the dummy. *The instant the dummy is in the dog's mouth*, stop the pinch. The dummy in the mouth turns off the discomfort of the ear pinch. What happens if the dog just stands there and screams? Grasp the dog's collar with your left hand, pinch the ear and drive the dog forward to the dummy with your left hand. *It is critical* that the ear pinch stops as soon as the dog grasps the dummy. Stopping the pinch too early or continuing too long will confuse the dog as to the connection between the secession of pain and grasping the dummy. Take a moment and think what you are going to do and say before beginning the lesson. Once the dog grasps the dummy, heel him off the table, give him lots of praise, come back to the table, test the grip and give the release command. Gradually work the dummy out to arm's length but still level with the eyes. When the dog is driving through the

dummy at arm's length, start lowering the dummy six to ten inches, and then work back out to arm's length. Anytime the dog refuses the dummy or balks, pinch the ear sharply until the dog re-grasps the dummy. Gradually phase out the ear pinch (done within the first arm's length) by just grasping the ear but do not pinch the ear so long as the dog does not hesitate to drive through and grasp the dummy. If he refuses, pinch the ear on the next rep and then hold the ear on the next rep, (no pinch) and drop the ear and just give the command on the next rep. The idea is to eliminate the pinch and holding the ear as soon as possible. The dog should go on command and grasp the dummy without hesitation.

The ear pinch. The handler's thumb is pinching the ear against the nametag on the collar.

All this time, you have held the dummy. Now for the first time, it is out of your hand and the dog must pick up a free-lying dummy from the table. You can provide some visual aid by point-ing to or touching the dummy with your finger. Since this is such a big step, grasp the ear in case you need to pinch it to get the dog to pick up the dummy off the table.

The reach and grasp phase, with the left hand ready to give an ear pinch upon refusal, the right hand holds the dummy six inches in front of the dog's mouth.

You are now ready to move to the third and final phase of the trained retrieve. The dog is now on a six- to eight-foot lead. Start the dog at the end of the table. Give him a *whoa* command, place the dummy about half the way down the table, and go back to the dog. Praise him for not moving. Give the *fetch* command. The dog will leave your side and pick up the dummy. Snap the lead and bring the dog back to you, check his grip, and give the release command. Continue this, gradually working the dummy out and down the ramp. Finally, place the dummy at the bottom of one ramp. Starting the dog at the base of the other ramp, give the *fetch* command with the dog on lead. The dog should pick up the dummy on the move and return directly to you, still on lead.

Start with a two-pound dummy and gradually increase the weight of the dummy to ten pounds. Mix this up with light dummies, to keep the dog from losing some of his enthusiasm. Always be ready to pinch the ear when increasing the weights. When the dog will pick up a ten-pound dummy at the end of the table and return with it, you are now ready to introduce cold, dead birds. Pigeons work well, just be sure that you do not use a badly shot up or bloody bird. Put the dog on *whoa* at one end of the table. Place the bird in the center of the table and return to the dog. Give the *fetch* command, giving an ear pinch if there is any hesitation. If the dog picks up the bird but is slow to return, use the lead to reel him in and give lots of praise.

When the dog is finished with the trained retrieve, he should hold anything on command.

When the dog is flawlessly going across the table, it is time to go to the yard. Starting with a dummy, gradually work out to twenty-five feet, the length of your check cord. Now is the time to put the dog into the position that you want before you take the bird from him. You can have him come directly to you: standing, sitting, or come to heel, etc. The important thing to remember is that eye contact is very important. When the dog has come to you, tilt his head up to have him look into your eyes. It is very hard for a dog to be disobedient while maintaining eye contact. Always check the grip and give the release command. When flawless with the dummy at twenty-five feet, introduce the cold, dead bird. Start close for the first rep, grasp the ear and gradually work out to twenty-five feet. Then switch to a fifty-foot line for dummies and birds. When the dog is flawless at these distances, you can start working him off lead, first with a dummy and then with a bird. Don't be afraid to give lavish praise as the dog returns. This will encourage greater enthusiasm and animation. You have now finished the trained retrieve. All that is needed from now on is lots of practice doing the real thing: Hunting!!

Whoa Training:
Phase One

The complete bird dog's goal in life is to go into the field, search, and find game birds. When he makes bird contact, he should immediately go on point and hold his point until his hunter comes up to him to flush and shoot the bird. A dog that is whoa trained will be steady throughout, from the moment he first scents the bird until the bird falls on the ground and his hunter gives him a release command to fetch it up. Whoa training is the foundation and the corner stone of all of your advanced training for a pointing dog. Once your dog is completely whoa trained, you will find that the other training sessions - steadiness by the blind, long retrieves - will be a lot easier. Here is what you will accomplish with a dog that is whoa trained:

- Your dog will hold birds and be steady to wing, flush, shot, and fall.
- Your dog will be under control and will stop on command. This is important when your dog is heading for danger, such as crossing a busy road or a railroad.
- Your dog will honor another dog's point.
- Your dog will hold still while you load your truck or when the vet is treating him for minor medical purposes. If your dog will lie still on a whoa command while he is getting x-rayed or stitched up, you may not have to have him anesthetized.

The time to start whoa training is after your dog has had a season in which he can learn as a young pup to boldly go out and find birds. This first season is a time that he learns through fun. Now that your young dog has built up a love for bird hunting and a strong hunting desire, you can start putting on the controls you will need to make your dog a part of a successful hunting team. There are many different methods and ways to whoa train your dog. Delmar Smith used the whoa post, George Hickoff uses his platform, and many people use a whoa training table. All of these methods work. However, the training technique that I like the best is the one developed and taught to me by Jeff Funke.

The first phase of training can be done in your own yard. You will need a pinch collar and a ten-foot lead rope. A pinch collar is a long collar that has flattened spikes sticking out of the inside. The tag end of the collar slips through a roller bar that allows the collar to be tightened and then loosened with ease. You will see some collars with pointed spikes. This is not a pinch collar; it is what is called a forced collar. If you buy a collar with sharp points you must flattened the spikes. Get a flat file and a hammer, lay the file on top of the points, and hit it with the hammer flattening the points. You do not want the collar to cut or hurt your dog. The training sessions will be stressful. They should be kept short: five to ten minutes twice a day.

In our training, we are going to use the same type of controls that the mother dog used on pup to control him when he was a young puppy. If you have had an opportunity to watch a mother dog with her young pups, you will see her use her mouth to quickly and firmly grasp her pup around the neck. By doing that, she has total control over the pup. The pup's reaction is to freeze. He is afraid to move until momma releas-

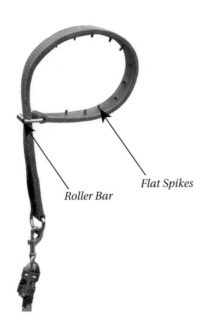

Flat Spikes

Roller Bar

es her hold. We are going to use the pinch collar and the lead to duplicate this same situation. You can precondition your dog to whoa training by using his mother's correction techniques. Before you feed your pup, grasp the top of his collar and pull up with a gentle, yet firm jerk. Make your pup stand until he relaxes and no longer fights against your grip before you allow him to feed. You can use this same technique before allowing your pup to do any number of activities such as retrieving, having a treat, or being released from a kennel or a pickup.

The collar should look like the letter"P' on your dog.

Put the pinch collar on your dog and snap the lead to the free end of the collar. The collar should look like the letter P when it is on your dog. The free end should be at the bottom pointing toward the ground. While your dog is standing still with the collar on, pull up on the collar and pinch him. Release the collar immediately and praise your dog. If your dog sits down when he is pinched take your foot, put it under this belly, and gently lift him up to a standing position After your dog stands when you pull up on the collar go to step two. Start walking your dog with a loose lead and the pinch collar loose around his neck. When your dog's mind is not on you or the collar quickly pull up on the lead, closing the collar firmly around his neck. Your dog should stop immediately. If he does, quickly release the collar and praise your dog with a verbal "good boy" and a pat on his shoulder. You want your dog to know that when he stops to the pressure of the collar on his neck he is doing the right thing. This part of the training is a conditioned response. The dog will learn to stop whenever he feels the collar tighten around his neck. At this stage your dog will learn faster without any verbal commands, except the praise when he performs correctly. We will introduce both a verbal and an electronic command at a later stage in the training.

If your dog attempts to move before you release him, pull up again on the rope, tightening the pinch collar. At this stage you want your dog to stand for about thirty seconds to a minute and then you want to start walking him again on a loose collar. Now you repeat the process. Walk your dog until his mind is on something else and he is not anticipating your pulling up on the collar. Talk softly to him and praise him while he is walking. You want him to relax. When he is relaxed, pull up on the lead and tighten the collar. When your dog stops, praise him. Three or four successful sequences are plenty for each session. Keep up this phase until your dog has a good understanding that he is to stop at once and stand when you tighten the collar and he is not to move out until you release him.

Most dogs will stop to the pinch collar. If your dog does not stop, he will fight the collar by pulling or jumping. If your dog fights the collar you can use the spin technique. You should already have your lead rope tight and the collar firmly around the dog's neck. Take both hands on the lead rope and lift the dog's front feet a few inches off the ground, spinning him around to your side. This takes only two or three seconds. It will not hurt your dog. Taking your dog suddenly off of his front feet and spinning him around makes him uncomfortable. Most dogs will stand still after one spin. When your dog stands still, praise him. If your dog still tries to fight the collar, spin him again. I have never had to spin a dog more than two times before he learned to stop. This technique should be used rarely and only as a last resort.

When your dog stops and stands every time for you, it is time to go to the next phase. In this phase, we want to tempt the dog to move. This process of whoa breaking is simply a series of increased levels of temptation. This is an important concept that many handlers never quite grasp. The more you tempt your dog during the training process the better trained he will be in the end. In actual hunting situations he will

Pulling up on the collar to "whoa" the dog.

be tempted to move many times. You want to make sure that your dog understands that no matter the temptation, he is not to move. Here your goal is to tempt your dog to make a mistake so that you can correct him. Each time you can cause your dog to make a mistake you have an opportunity to make a correction, thereby furthering the dog's understanding of the whoa command. Your dog will encounter a lot of distractions in the bird field. He will have birds flush wild, run on him, and he will hear other shots being fired close to him. All of these distractions will tempt him to break. During your whoa training you want to expose your dog to a number of different distractions. When he breaks, you have an opportunity to correct him. You want him to be totally steady.

In this stage, repeat the sequence of walking your dog and stopping him with the pinch collar. Now back up from him, holding the lead rope. When you get to the end of the lead, gently pull the rope toward you. This will tempt your dog to start walking or coming to you. If he does, quickly go to him and pull up on the rope and tighten the pinch collar. Your dog will soon learn not to move even when you pull on the rope. You will find that he will staunch up and resist being pulled. That's great. That's what you want. When he stands to your pulling, praise him. Another method to tempt your dog is to walk around him while holding the lead rope. When you get behind your dog he will be tempted to move. He wants to see where you are. When he turns, pull up on the rope and stop him. Remember, do this in silence. Don't confuse the dog by giving verbal commands at this stage. However, you can use the basic, silent command of holding your hand up, palm facing the dog, to reinforce the fact hat he should stay put.

Another good temptation is to take one of your dog's favorite toys, or his training dummy. When you have whoa'd your dog with the collar, toss the toy or dummy out in front of him. His natural instinct will be to rush to get it. When this happens, stop him with the collar. Continue tossing objects for him during the training sessions until he will remain still. Do not end the session unless he is successfully standing through the temptation. When your dog is reliably standing through all kinds of distractions, you are ready to move on to the next phase of whoa training, using live birds.

Tempting the dog to move by pulling on the collar. Note the dog resisting.

Hunhaven Sprig

Belle remains steady after a short tug on the pinch collar, note the bird in the air.

Whoa Training:
Phase Two

Now that your dog is stopping at the pinch and resisting temptations to move, it is time to introduce him to birds. This is simply an extension of phase one, only now you are going to teach him to whoa and remain steady when he makes bird contact. You are also going to tempt him to move by using live birds. For this phase of training you will need:

- Pinch collar
- Ten-foot check cord
- Thirty-foot check cord
- Live birds
- Blank gun

- Release traps
- Bird bag
- Popper shells
- Live ammunition
- Helpers

As soon as the dog sees the bird on the ground, give a cautionary pinch with the collar as a reminder to stand still.

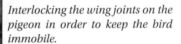

Interlocking the wing joints on the pigeon in order to keep the bird immobile.

Pigeons are the best birds to use in the early part of this training. They fly well and since you won't be shooting birds until the end of this phase the pigeons, if trained, will fly back to their pen and can be used again. At the end of this phase you will be shooting live birds. It is best to start with pigeons and finish with either quail or chukars.

Ideally you should use a training area different from the one you used in the first part of whoa training. A grass field, similar to the type of field the dog would be in when hunting, is great. Put the pinch collar on your dog and snap on the ten-foot check cord. Put four to six pigeons in your bird bag. Walk your dog into the field, stop him with a pinch, and then throw a bird up into the air in front of him. When he moves, correct him with the pinch collar. Repeat throwing birds in front of him until he stands without moving. Each time you stop your dog with a pinch and he stands while the pigeon flies away, release your dog with a tap on the head and your release command. Praise him every time he stops and stands. You can repeat this procedure twice a day, but make sure that there is at least an hour between sessions. Repeat throwing birds in front of your dog in these ten-minute sessions until he will no longer try to chase the bird.

Now it is time to introduce the gun. Repeat the step of throwing birds in front of your dog but, when the bird takes flight, fire a blank gun into the air. If your dog moves, correct him with the pinch collar. The sound of the gun is an added temptation for the dog to break. Repeat this step in several locations until your dog no longer tries to break and chase the bird at the shot.

After your dog is whoaing and standing still at the flight of the bird and the shot, you can increase the temptation by using wing-tied pigeons on the ground. A wing-tied pigeon is a pigeon with its wings locked together. Grasp the wings and hold them so the tips are facing straight up and the tops of the wings are touching each other. Now with one wing in each hand, place the front of the left wing behind the right wing so that the contact point is at the first joint of the right wing. The first joint is where the wing meets the body. Continue with one more lock by placing the front of the right wing behind the left wing so that the second contact point is at the second joint on the left wing. This wing-tie does not hurt the bird, but the bird is immobilized and cannot fly, but it can walk.

Take your dog on the thirty-foot check cord and put him on whoa with a stop, using the pinch collar. Place a wing-tied pigeon on the ground eight to ten feet in front of your dog. You can do this yourself, however a helper is a plus. As soon as your dog sees the bird, give him a cautionary pinch. This is still a non-verbal communication on the correction but some verbal praise is fine. In this stage you are conditioning

After the dog is standing still at the flush, phase in the gun. Of course, the gun should have been introduced well before whoa training.

the dog to stand while you move in front of him toward the bird. With these vulnerable birds lying on the ground most dogs become aggressive and try to grab the bird. When your dog moves, stop him with the pinch collar. When your dog allows you to walk in front of him so that you can reach the bird, you or your helper can untie the wings and let the bird fly away. Be ready to administer a correction. Each time you repeat this step you should increase the temptation by fidgeting with the bird in front of the dog. Kick toward the bird simulating a flushing attempt. Move the bird around with your foot. Pick the bird up and toss it closer to the dog without flying it. Do anything you can to tempt your dog to move. Remember the quality of your dog's whoa training is a function of the amount of temptation that he can overcome.

Now you will have your dog point birds. You can use wing-tied birds, dizzied birds, or birds in a launcher. Automatic launchers work best especially when you train alone. Take three or four birds and place them in the field in a line pattern. Bring your dog up on a ten-foot rope attached to the pinch collar. Walk your dog downwind of the birds so that when he hits the scent, he will turn and be perpendicular to the bird in the launcher. The instant your dog scents the bird, snap the pinch collar and give him a correction, so that he will freeze in his tracks. Do not allow your dog to take a single step after scenting the bird. You have been praising your dog all along; now step it up a bit. While your dog is on point, really stroke him. Stack his tail, pet his side, style him up, and verbally praise him; making him look and feel good. Move ahead of your dog and flight the bird. You should also fire a blank gun or a shotgun with a popper load. If your dog stands through the whole process without receiving a correction, move him on to the next bird by lifting him slightly off the ground and carrying him a few feet in the direction you want him to go. This is done for several reasons. First, you do not want to encourage your dog to move off point. Second, lifting your dog and moving him will prevent the dog from lunging at the old scent spot. Repeat these sessions, working your dog on three or four birds each time. Two or three sessions a week is ideal. Make corrections on your dog as necessary. When your dog is standing and allowing you to move in to flush the bird and fire a shot, it is time to increase the temptation. Use launchers to flight a double and then a triple while your dog stands. On occasion, flight a bird as soon as your dog scents it. When the bird flies, give him a pinch. This will keep your dog sharp. He thinks he made a mistake and got too close to the bird or didn't slam the point with enough intensity.

In the next stage you will shoot the birds for the dog. The sequence is the same; three or four birds in a line with your dog on the check cord. When your dog points the bird, walk ahead, flush the bird and shoot it. If your dog moves, make a correction with the pinch collar. Repeat this sequence until your dog is flawless. Then shoot a double. Do not let your dog retrieve the birds at this point. Make him stand while you or your helper go out and pick up the bird. This will teach your dog to whoa and stand still through wing, shot, and fall. Most people prefer to have their dogs break at shot to retrieve the bird. This is fine during an actual hunting situation. However, dogs anticipate everything. If a dog has only been taught to be steady to flush, he will start to anticipate the flush and often times he will move to take out the bird before the flush. A dog that is not trained to be steady through the fall will generally move when the bird moves. He will often break in and chase birds before you have a chance at a clear shot. By training your dog to be steady through the entire process - wing, shot, and fall - you avoid this problem. A fully broke dog is more obedient and more confident in the field. When your dog will point and stand planted birds, and let you flush, shoot, and pick up the bird, you are ready to incorporate the verbal *whoa* command and make the transition from the pinch collar to the electronic collar.

Flushing the bird from a launcher is the next big temptation.

Chuck and Baron

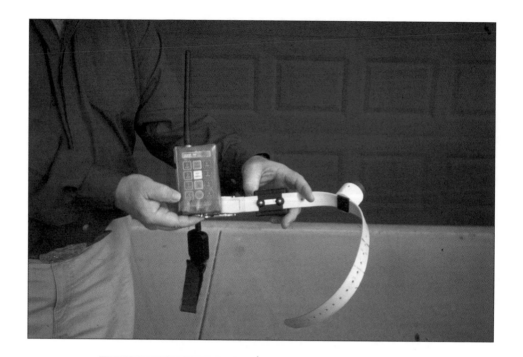

Whoa Training:
Phase Three

When your dog will point and stand for planted birds, and let you flush, shoot, and pick up the bird, you are ready to incorporate the verbal *whoa* command. To teach the verbal *whoa* command, go back to the beginning. Start with the ten-foot check cord attached to the pinch collar and walk your dog using the verbal *whoa* command at the same time you give your dog a pinch. Repeat each of the phases, tempting your dog with dummies, wing-tied birds, and live birds. At each stage give the verbal *whoa* command, and then simultaneously give the dog a pinch. Stay with each stage until your dog associates the *whoa* command with stopping and standing still. To bolster the dog's understanding of the verbal *whoa* command, you should teach him to stop while coming toward you when you call him. Place your dog on whoa and walk out thirty to forty feet. Command and coax your dog to come toward you. When he gets half way to you, throw your traffic cop hand up and command, Whoa. If the dog stops, go to him and praise him. Repeat this lesson several times and vary the distance and location until you are sure your dog understands the *whoa* command. If your dog does not stop immediately on your *whoa* command, go to him and lift him up and put him back to the precise spot he was when you gave him the command and shake him up a bit by pulling on his collar. Keep increasing the distance until your dog will whoa immediately on your command.

Adding the verbal "whoa" command as your dog comes back to you along with the raised hand. The traffic cop signal.

Now you have a dog that will whoa and stand without a command when he sees a bird fly or scents a bird. He will stand and let you go in front of him and flush and shoot the bird. He will then wait for your release command to fetch the bird for you. You now have a totally whoa broke dog.

There is one other step that I encourage you to use. That is to train your dog to whoa using an electric collar. It is the single most effective way of communicating with your dog while in the field hunting birds. If you have gone this far in training your dog, it does not take that much more time to whoa train your dog on the e-collar. During actual hunting situations it is far easier to control your dog using an e-collar.

The purpose of the e-collar is to be able to communicate with your dog in the field. The e-collar allows you to give your dog commands at a distance and will ultimately increase your productivity in the field by insuring immediate response to your commands. The e-collar will also allow you to confidently hunt your dog at increased range, thereby increasing your productivity by providing more opportunity for bird contact. It is not a tool for punishment. If your dog is introduced properly to the e-collar he will be happy to have it on. My dogs get excited and eagerly push toward me when they see the collar. They all want the collar put on them because they associate the collar with bird hunting, their number one love in life.

Before we get to the final phase of whoa training, a review of the basics of using an e-collar is in order. These rules are important because the e-collar, while being an effective communication tool, can be very dangerous and can ruin a dog faster than all other training tools combined.

- **Proper fit:** The collar should fit around the dog's neck with the contact points on the underside of his neck near the throat. This is the most sensitive spot on a dog. The collar should be snug to ensure good skin contact, but not so tight that it inhibits the dog's breathing. If it is too loose, you will not get proper skin contact and you will get inconsistent results. Also, electric collars that are fit too loose will chafe the skin around the dog's neck.
- **Sensitivity:** It is critical that you determine your dog's sensitivity level. What you are looking for is the dog's Minimum Response Level (MRL). Ninety percent of your training will be at this MR Level. Put the e-collar on your dog and start at the lowest level. Look for any response from your dog: a turn of the head, a low yelp, a tensing of his shoulders. Any physical sign at all is the level that you want to use for training. Most dogs will respond at levels one, two or three.
- **Too Hot:** Do not use the collar at a level that hurts your dog. You are using a level that is too high if your dog cries or screams. This level is only used for avoidance training, such as for deer or poisonous snakes. Dogs do not learn very well at this level. They become easily stressed and confused and learning is impeded. If you continue too hot for very many repetitions, you may create problems that cannot be fixed.
- **Sight:** Never electrically stimulate your dog unless you can see what your dog is doing. If you shock your dog while he is out of sight, you may be punishing him for doing something good. If he is pointing a bird and you shock him, you may cause him to blink birds.
- **Instant Reaction:** As with any correction, never stimulate unless you can do so within two seconds of negative behavior. Delayed corrections will create huge problems that are tough to fix. Do not worry if you miss a correction – you can always set up a similar situation another day. You may not be able to fix a problem that you have created by improper use of the e-collar.
- **Learned Commands:** Only use the e-collar to reinforce a known command. Other than pure avoidance training where you may shock a dog at a very hot level for chasing deer or encountering a poisonous snake, you should only use the e-collar to reinforce a previously taught command. There are techniques for teaching directly with an e-collar, but they are dangerous and should be avoided by the average bird dog trainer.
- **Praise:** As with any correction, praise your dog after he responds correctly.
- **Adult Dogs Only:** Do not use the collar on a puppy—basically, a dog under one year of age. Puppies should go through their first year of life thinking everything is a positive learning experience. You can use an e-collar on very young dogs with adequate results, but I avoid doing so whenever possible. You will use the e-collar for very specific training on adult dogs that have already built a great deal of hunting desire and are totally confident on birds and in the water. If you use the e-collar on a puppy, you run the risk of making a mistake. A bad mistake on a pup may ruin the dog forever.

Finally, when in doubt about an action, don't take it. Simple rule: If you are not sure about whether or not you should be using the electric collar at a given instant, do not use it. You can always access the situation later or get the advice of a professional. It is better to err on the side of caution when it comes to the electronic collar.

The e-collar when properly used, does not take any long term enthusiasm out of your dog. And it will give you a measure of long-distance control. Chukar steady to flush.

Chukar brought up on a bird with the long lead, and with the e-collar ready to remind him to stop if he moves.

Whoa Training:
Phase Four

In the first three phases, you learned how to use a pinch collar to whoa train your dog. You advanced through various stages until your dog was steady to wing and shot, and you could also stop him with a verbal *whoa*. The ideal situation is to be able to communicate your desire for your dog to whoa and have the ability to do it at a distance without using your voice. Many wild birds will flush at the sound of a human voice. The e-collar, if introduced properly, is the ideal tool to accomplish this task. Make no mistake. We are not using the e-collar to punish or discipline your dog. When a dog is properly introduced to the collar, he will be eager to have it put on him. At the end of the third phase, we reviewed the basic rules for the humane use of the e-collar.

In order to make the transition from the pinch collar to the e-collar, you will go back to the beginning. Remember, you started the dog on the pinch collar and a short lead. You walked the dog and stopped him by pulling up on the pinch collar. As soon as he stopped, you praised him and then gave him a release command and walked him again. You repeated stopping him five or six times with the pinch collar at each session.

Now put both the pinch collar and the e-collar on your dog and start walking him with a short lead. Stop him by first pulling up on the pinch collar and, a second after the collar is tightened, press the e-collar on the lowest stimulation level. This level should only give the dog a vibration, and it should also have a sound. Remember, with just the tone and the vibration, you are not shocking the dog. Your dog knows to stop when he feels the pressure of the pinch collar. We are now tying the two together: pinch, low vibration. By repeating the sequence and the sessions, your dog will soon learn to stop when he hears and feels the e-collar.

After your dog is stopping to the pinch and e-collar on the short lead, repeat the sequence with the thirty-foot lead, using the pinch, e-collar sequence. When your dog becomes used to the e-collar, it is time to move on to the next phase. Go back to the short, ten-foot lead. Keep both collars on the dog. Walk your dog and try to stop him using only the e-collar. If the dog stops on command, lavish praise on him. You want him to understand and make the transition to stop to the tone on the e-collar. If he does not stop with just the e-collar, use the pinch and the e-collar together. Each dog is different. Some dogs make the change quickly; others take longer. Do not get frustrated. Your dog will learn to stop on the e-collar. Just keep repeating the sessions. When your dog is always stopping with only the e-collar command, advance to the thirty-foot lead. Again, keep both collars on the dog. Your dog should make a quick transition to stopping with the longer lead.

Now we are going to introduce birds into the training sessions. Use homing pigeons and tie their wings, dropping them in a field with short grass. Keep your dog on the thirty-foot lead with both collars. Bring your dog up to see the first bird. As soon as he sees the bird, try to stop him using only the e-collar. If he stops, give him praise. If he does not stop with the e-collar, use both the pinch and the e-collar. Keep the sessions short, exposing your dog to three different birds a session. When your dog stops consistently with the e-collar, it is time to increase the dog's temptation to move. Bring your dog up to the bird and stop him with the e-collar. When the dog stops, have a helper move the bird. He can pick it up and toss it a few feet in front of the dog. If the dog moves, stop him with the e-collar. At each stage, when your dog stops with the e-collar, gradually increase the temptation for him to break. Your dog learns best by making mistakes and receiving a correction. Now have your helper untie the wings and let the bird fly away. If your dog moves, stop him with the e-collar. In many cases the temptation of a live, moving bird is too much to stop the dog on the e-collar's lowest level. You might have to use the next level up to stop him. Make sure that you praise your dog every time he stops for you. You want to reinforce in his mind that he is doing the right thing by stopping immediately when he hears and feels the vibration of the collar.

Now it is time to run your dog in the field with no birds. Remember you want to have a dog that will whoa whenever you command him, not just during bird contact. When your dog is running out in front of you twenty-five to forty yards, try to stop him with a low level stimulation. He should stop. If not, raise the level of stimulation one level. You can also use your verbal *whoa* to stop him. When he stops, give him both verbal praise and a pat on the side.

In the next stage take a bird bag with five to six homing pigeons, your dog with the e-collar on, and go into a bird field. When your dog is searching out in front of you and looking toward you, take a bird out of the bag and let it fly. As soon as your dog sees the bird he will most likely start to chase it. Hit the e-collar and stop him. Praise him for stopping and let him search again. Repeat letting birds fly until the dog stops at the sight of a bird in flight. This might take two or three sessions before the dog stops to the sight of the flighted bird. Do not get frustrated. Keep the sessions up until your dog stops and is steady.

Now add the sound of a shotgun to each session. Have a helper carry a gun and shoot a blank in the air when you release the bird. You do not want to kill a bird at this stage. You want the dog to see the bird, hear the gun, and stop. At first, use the e-collar to stop him. Your dog will soon begin to stop without the e-collar signal. He will learn to stop at the sight of the bird and the sound of the gun. He is learning by repetition and by your praise that you want him to stop when he sees birds or hears the sound of the gun or whenever he hears and feels the e-collar at the lowest level.

During the next stage of whoa training you will plant pigeons in bird launchers. Three launchers, spread out in a bird field, work well for each training session. Send your dog into the field and give him your command to search/hunt. When he smells the birds he should stop and point. When he is pointing, flight the bird out of the launcher. If your dog moves or starts to chase, use the e-collar at the lowest level to stop him. Praise your dog for stopping. Release him and let him continue to hunt. At

When making the transition to the e-collar to reinforce the whoa command, go back to the long lead and, for a time, use both.

the next bird contact, release the bird and fire a blank gun in the air. If he moves, use the collar to stop him. When the dog points the third bird, flight it and kill it for the dog. Make sure he is steady to flight and the sound of the gun before doing this. When the bird is dead, release him and let him retrieve the bird. This is his reward for being steady. During any of these sessions be prepared to stop your dog with the e-collar if necessary.

Now plant birds in the cover without launchers. You will need a helper. Have your helper carry the transmitter. Tell him to stop the dog with the e-collar if he moves or tries to chase the bird. You should carry a gun, and when your dog finds and points the birds, you go in to flush the bird and shoot it. In this final stage you are duplicating an actual bird-hunting situation. When your dog does everything right, let him retrieve the bird as his reward. By following all of these stages of whoa training, your dog will be conditioned through each stage to stop and be steady, even with increased temptations. That is the essence of whoa training. Your dog now has learned to whoa any time he sees a bird, hears a gun, or when you use the e-collar to stop him even when there is no bird contact. When a dog has been taught to stop on command, both verbal and with the e-collar, he understands what you expect of him and he is happy to do it. The dog makes the connection between the birds and the collar. He has learned to hunt with you and work with you as part of the team. You have used the e-collar with low stimulation. The dog learned by association, not by pain. You now have a fully finished dog capable of learning and being trained to do anything. This whoa training method is a generic method that you can use to train a dog in any situation in a short period of time.

The dog nearing the end of his whoa-training should allow you to walk in front of him, flush and shoot the bird without moving. The e-collar is your backup in case he lapses.

Chukar is a steady dog that will hold birds, no matter how long it takes for you to catch up. You just need to trust him.

A Versatile Hunting Dog's Comfortable Range

What is your dog's comfortable range when hunting birds? That is both a real question and a real problem for many versatile dog owners. I frequently get phone calls from versatile dog owners describing their problems with range. Jim McDermott just wrote a marvelous book entitled *A Hunter, His Bird Dog and Their Quest for a Comfortable Range*. I will quote some of his comments about his struggle to achieve the right balance in range with Speck, his English setter.

I have also asked John Crozier and Ken Marsh to share their thoughts on a comfortable range for versatile dogs. John is a professional versatile dog trainer whose dogs hunt ruffed grouse in the woods of Pennsylvania and sharptail grouse in the western prairies, and Ken is a professional pointing dog trainer in Montana, who also trains a number of versatile dogs. John finds that most new hunting dog owners make a mistake when, the minute their dog makes a nice long, bold cast, they call him back by using the whistle and often the e-collar. The dog soon learns that whenever he ranges out, he gets punished. Now the dog is afraid to leave his handler's side. A dog that is constantly hacked in close will never develop the confidence to establish its genetic range and potential as a bird finder.

Depending upon the cover and the bird being hunted, Chukar will adjust his range.

Range is the distance that a hunting dog goes out from his hunter to find birds. The ideal bird dog learns to adjust his range to fit the bird being hunted and the terrain. John, Ken, and I agree that the genetic makeup of a dog greatly determines his range. A puppy from a line of close-working grouse dogs is more likely to have a much shorter range than a pup from a western line of dogs whose ancestors have primarily hunted prairie birds and have been bred to have a much bigger search. John advises hunters to pick a pup from a breeding program and line that matches their hunting pace and style.

Exposure and training will also have an influence on your dog's search. Getting your young pup into a variety of cover and different species of game birds will go a long way in teaching him how to vary his search and range to successfully find birds. Versatile dog owners have an advantage over other pointing dog breeds that are bred to hunt only one way and one bird. An example would be the big-running English pointers used to hunt quail in Texas. The versatile breeds were developed to hunt a variety of birds, including waterfowl. Over the generations they have learned to become more adaptable in their hunting ability. They seem to catch on more quickly that they need to vary their range with the type of bird they are hunting. The versatile gun dog is usually a very friendly dog that bonds strongly with his owner. Ken believes that the versatile dog is a very humanized dog that wants to please his owner. He finds that the versatile dog will work better as a team with his owner, and adjust his range more readily to the range his owner prefers. Recently, Ken trained a versatile dog for a hunter who had a physical disability; he was not able to walk the fields as quickly as most hunters. After he bonded with his new dog, the dog quickly learned his hunter's limitations and decreased his range so that he was finding birds that his hunter could get to and shoot. Spend time and bond with your new pup. A strong bond between you and your dog will make it easier for both of you to find a comfortable range that allows your dog to use his full talents to search and find birds, and at the same time work with you so that the birds he finds, points, and holds will be within range for you to get to the bird and shoot it.

One of the biggest mistakes you can make is to start putting controls on your young dog too soon. Ken, John, and I all like to give a pup his first year in the field with minimal controls. We want him to develop his desire and search to the fullest extent. You can always put the controls on later. It is very difficult to get a dog to extend his range; it is much easier to rein him in. Instead of putting too many controls on your young pup, watch him as he learns to search. Read your dog. Learn the signals he is sending you: the way he runs, holds his head, the body language he expresses when he finds birds. Knowing your dog will help you in your advanced training. Here is the problem you face when you start controls too soon. Jim McDermott wrote,

> *"For three seasons... we marched forward in a hail of earsplitting noise, with the obedient bird dog precisely navigating the cover in response to the nit-picking demands of his control-freak handler... It was as if we had given up real hunting...as our experiences afield grew increasingly artificial."*

Even when he's in the distance, Chukar is still hunting for me. Our relationship and bonding will cause him to hunt with me as part of a team.

After your dog has had his first year in the field you will want to whoa train him. A dog that is completely whoa trained will hold his birds no matter how far he ranges in the field. A big ranging dog is an advantage in hunting many game birds. Prairie grouse and chukars live in big country. A dog that gets out in the field will find more birds for you than a dog that hunts close. The key to success is a dog that is whoa trained and will pin and hold the birds until you get to him.

The ideal situation is one in which the hunter and his dog hunt together as a team. Each of them knows his job and what the other expects of him. Both the dog and his hunter must learn to trust each other. Often the hunter has the most trouble trusting his dog. He has this pre-conceived notion as to how he wants his dog to hunt and cover the ground. He believes he knows better than his dog where the birds are and how to handle them. If that is the case, then who needs a dog? Over the years I have found that my dog's ability to find and handle birds successfully is far greater than my own. I have learned to trust my dogs. During my last hunt this year I knocked a pheasant down and my hunting buddy said, "The bird is dead right in front of you". My dog went to where the bird fell and quickly moved on, tracking the supposedly dead bird another forty yards, where she caught it. My partner kept telling me to call my dog back. I knew from past experience that my dog knew far better then me where the bird was. This is just one example of placing trust in your dog. If I had called my dog back and made her continue to search the area where the bird fell, we probably would not have recovered it. Jim talks about trust in his book,

> "As Speck charged through the cover in pursuit of another rooster, it felt good to know that the whistle wasn't needed. For a long time I had assumed that by continually managing his search, with the whistle and voice command, and hand signals, I had been teaching him to hunt within range. But he was demonstrating, once more, that by letting go of my desire to keep him fully in check I could erase the constant need for him to be controlled.... Speck was coming into his own: all I had to do now, it seemed, was to trust him."

It takes time for you and your versatile dog to develop the style and range that works for both of you. Be patient, take the time to bond with your dog, let him develop his hunting ability and range, and learn to trust him. The end result will be a dog that has developed as a great hunting dog and the pleasure of working together as a bird hunting team.

"Speck floated through the grass without effort, moving fast but gracefully, putting more and more space between us until he had reached the line we had drawn together in the process of working out a comfortable range. That had not been a matter simply of training regimes...It had something to do with teaching and direction on my part, but there was more to it then that. It was also a matter of hunting together..." Jim concludes his book with this thought, *"Three months ago I had imagined that a calamity would overtake us. I had been more than anxious... I had been afraid. Now I knew that Speck was with me. I understood that, even when he raced out of sight, we were hunting together all the time."*

Chukar is steady while I go in to flush the bird.

Chuck and Duke on a goose hunt in North Dakota.

A little pep talk before the hunt starts can get everyone on the same page.

How to Handle Your Dog in the Field

Many bird hunters miss opportunities to harvest more birds because they make mistakes handling their bird dog while he is in the hunting field. After your dog has had one hunting season as a pup and another season in which you have put the controls on him, you should be hunting as a team. A well-trained dog that has the natural instincts to hunt hard and has a good nose needs very little handling in the field.

My experience is that the hunter makes most of the mistakes made in the field, not the dog. There are several common mistakes that a handler makes in handling his dog.

The biggest error is trying to over direct and control the dog. Many hunters try to micro manage their dog. Instead of letting the dog search the cover, they are constantly giving their dogs repetitive, vocal commands. I remember one case where I was hunting quail with a guide and his dog. We had a wounded bird down. The dog was attempting to find the bird. The guide kept up a constant *Hunt Dead* command. I lost count when he hit the fiftieth time he gave his dog the same command in less than five minutes.

The best advice a professional dog trainer gave me was to "keep my mouth shut". He said, "Chuck, let your dogs work. They are doing fine. You are giving them too many commands that will only confuse them." Game birds are very sensitive to human sound. I have watched this phenomenon many times as a group of hunters pull into the end of a CRP field. They are talking to each other; slamming car doors, as they get ready to hunt. I have watched the other end of the field with binoculars and observed pheasants running out, making their escape. They recognized the sound of cars and human voices as bad news.

Many hunters do not trust their dogs and keep their dogs almost at their feet. A pointing dog is genetically built to reach out to search for and find birds. Trust your dog if he has been properly whoa trained. He will hold point until you get to him. Overuse of the e-collar, shocking the dog to try and rein him in, is another major mistake. The end result is a dog that is afraid to search for birds. He soon becomes a boot licker.

As we discussed in an earlier chapter, it is important to be able to read your dog. It is extremely important to know when your dog is making game. It is also important to know when your dog is tracking a wounded bird. Too many times a hunter calls his dog off birds. I also watch my dogs very closely from the time they are young puppies as to how they act when they are working birds. Every dog is different and will work birds in its own way. The position of the head, the action of the dog's body and his tail are all distinct signs that will signal you that he is working a bird. As you get to know your dog better you will be able to tell when he is close to a bird, and when he is ready to point. The better you read your dog, the better you will be working as a

Hand signals work well when your dog is in sight of you. The lack of noise also helps in not spooking the birds.

Chukar is cruising way out looking for Huns. The e-collar, particularly the tone, is great for communicating with your dog in this situation.

Chukar is on point. I use the tone-only button to let him know that I see him and am coming.

team with little or no verbal communication. I have learned from experience not to continue to call my dog back when I can't see him. Last year I was hunting the prairies for sharptail and Huns with Chukar, who went over a ridge and out of sight. I called him several times and he did not come back. I then started looking for him. It took me ten minutes to find him. He was on point in the bottom of a shallow coulee. I know he heard me call but he had enough sense and training to stay on point. I went up to him, flushed a covey of Huns, and got two. This incident reinforced my principle of not constantly calling my dog when he is out of sight. In most cases he is either working birds or on point.

Tracking a wounded bird is another situation in which hunters tend not to trust their dog. You shoot a pheasant and it falls straight down into the high cover. You are convinced that the bird is stone dead. Your dog goes in to retrieve and does not come back with the bird. Soon your dog is heading away from where the bird fell. Now you call him back because you are sure the bird is right where he fell; your dog just missed him. Your dog searches the area again and then starts to track. The dog knows that the bird is just wounded and has run away. Trust your dog. Let him track and find the bird and bring it back to you. In some cases my dogs have tracked a wounded bird for hundreds of yards, caught it and retrieved it for me.

The best hunting team in the field is one in which the hunter and bird dog are connected with each other like a large flexible rubber band. Whether your dog is hunting close in CRP or ranging out on the prairies, the two of you are working together. "The bird hunter watches only the dog and always knows where the dog is, whether or not visible," Aldo Leopold wrote. This is what you want to achieve.

Here are some suggestions as to how to communicate with your dog in the field. Remember: The fewer commands you give, the better. The best way to start your hunt so both you and your dog are in sync is to set your dog up at the edge of the bird field, whoa him, and then give him a release command to go hunt. If your dog is in sight, you can use nonverbal hand signals to change his directions. You can also use a whistle to give your dog commands. I like to use my whistle sparingly. I only use it when I know my dog is out of range of the e-collar and I want him to come to me.

The e-collar is a great tool to communicate with your dog. I do not mean using it to shock your dog. The more advanced e-collars have a button for tone only. They also have a beeper. You can keep the beeper on continually or set it so that it will only beep when the dog is on point. This is called the silent mode. You can also activate the beeper so you can locate your dog. Here is how I use the e-collar in the field: When my dog goes on point I will hear the beeper. At that time I press the tone-only button. This lets my dog know that I am aware that he is on point and to hold point. I am coming to him. When I am sure I have located my dog, I will turn the beeper off. I do not want to disturb the birds.

When I want to locate my dog, I simply press the button that activates the beeper. It will beep one time and let me know where my dog is in the field. If I want my dog to come back to me, I can activate the beeper and keep it going for thirty seconds or more. This alerts the dog to swing around and come back to me. You can start using this system when you are using the collar to whoa train your dog. I have found that the dogs catch on quickly. If you are hunting more than one dog and one dog goes on point and the beeper starts, the other dogs will run to the dog with the beeping collar. They have learned that the beeper means birds.

We have talked a great deal about what your dog should do for you in the field. You also have a responsibility to do your part in the field. Stay alert and watch your dog. When your dog goes on point go to him quickly, flush the bird, and kill it. A good bird hunter owes it to himself and his dogs to be a good shot. Practice in the off-season. Everyone misses a bird now and then. However, it is not fair to your dog for you to miss bird after bird. When that happens, I have seen dogs that quit pointing and start flushing birds. Why should they point and hold a bird if you are not going to be able to hit it?

The ideal team of hunter and bird dog is built over a period of time. It starts when your dog is a young puppy. It begins with bonding with your dog. Spending time with him; taking the time to train him properly; and, most important, trusting your dog. And, finally, you need to make sure that you deserve to be trusted by him.

Training Your Dog for Water Retrieves

Hunting ducks in the morning and upland birds in the afternoon with your dog is one of the major reasons more and more people are buying one of the many versatile breeds of pointing dogs. Owning two or more dogs is not only expensive, it can also be difficult to do in many urban areas due to laws, lack of space, etc. A good versatile dog that hunts both upland birds and waterfowl solves this problem.

Even if you only hunt upland birds, I still believe that it is a great advantage for your dog to be able to swim and retrieve game birds in the water. Most of the pheasant hunting I do in Montana is on the river bottoms. Every year I have shot at least one pheasant that falls into the water or lands across the water. In that situation you have three options: A) leave the bird, which is unacceptable; B) wade or swim in the water to retrieve your downed bird; or C) let your dog retrieve the bird for you. Personally, I prefer the third option. Before I owned German wirehaired pointers, I had an English setter and also an English pointer. They both loved the water and had no problem retrieving birds in the water for me.

The best way to introduce your dog to the water is when he is a very young puppy. I get all my puppies in the water when they are seven to eight weeks old. During the off-season, I run all of my dogs several times a week to keep them in condition. As part of their conditioning I take them to a pond and throw dummies into the water for

Start your dog off with fun fetches in the water for dummies.

Swimming after a flightless duck further intensifies the prey chase drive.

them to retrieve. My dogs love this. It is the highlight of their conditioning session. It is an easy transition to teach a dog that already loves to retrieve dummies in the water to learn to retrieve birds in the water. I have versatile dogs because I love to hunt ducks. I want my dogs to be proficient in finding and retrieving ducks in the water.

In the first stage of training a dog for water retrieves, I get a duck and either tape its wings to its body or pull the primary feathers out of one wing. The duck can still swim and walk, but it cannot fly. I have my dog on a lead by the edge of the pond and I have an assistant show him the duck. Then my helper will toss the duck out into the water. As soon as the duck is about twenty-five yards from the bank, I let my dog loose and give him a *fetch* command. Almost every dog will jump into the water and start chasing the duck. Many young dogs will bark in excitement. When the dog catches the duck, I praise him and call him back. When he brings the duck to me, I praise him again. After one or two duck chases, when the dog is pulling on the lead to go after the duck, it is time to introduce the gun. Now I let the duck get further out into the water before I release my dog. At this time, the helper puts a popper load into his shotgun and points the gun into the air. When the duck is out in the water, the helper fires the gun. After the shot, I release the dog and tell him to fetch.

Now the dog is beginning to associate the sound of the gun with retrieving a bird in the water. A popper load is a shotgun shell with a primer and a very light load of powder. There is no shot in the load. Most sporting good stores or major hunting catalogs carry them. They normally run about $10.00 for a box of twenty-five shells.

To simulate a real hunting situation, I have the helper go to the far side of the pond with the duck. In this situation, I have the shotgun with the popper load. Bringing the dog up to the pond, I have the handler throw the duck into the water. When the duck is in the air I fire a popper load, and then release the dog to fetch the duck. To add to the realism of the hunting situation, you can also put some decoys in the water in front of where you release your dog for the retrieve. You want your dog to get used to seeing decoys and swimming through them. Let your dog check out the decoys. At first he might try to retrieve the decoys; however he will soon learn the difference between a decoy and a real bird.

You can also use a pheasant or other upland game bird for the water retrieve. Follow the same procedure, but have your helper toss an upland bird into the water. You want your dog to understand that when you bring him to the water whether, it's a pond, lake, or stream, and tell him to fetch, he will be convinced that there is a game bird, either waterfowl or upland, in the water for him to retrieve.

With the handler and the bird across the pond, you can start to introduce the gun.

When the dog understands that firing a gun and giving him a search command means there is a wounded duck in the water he will make a tenacious search over the entire body of water and adjoining land until he finds the duck, a bird that he did not see fall. This is the ultimate water performance in a versatile dog and something to be proud of.

The final stage in training for water retrieves is the blind retrieve. In this situation, a duck has fallen into the water and disappeared into heavy cover, such as cattails or high grass along the shore. Even if you and your dog saw where the duck fell, that does not mean it will stay there. If it is wounded it will swim away. This is graduate training for your dog. An outstanding dog will go into the water on your command, without seeing the bird, and hunt the entire pond until he picks up the scent cone of the bird and follows it, finds the bird, and brings it to you.

A bird scent will stay on the top of the water just like it stays on the ground. A dog's nose will pick up the scent, recognize it and track it, just like he tracks birds on the ground. We start this training by bringing your dog up to the edge of the pond. Tell him to sit and have your helper throw a taped duck into the water. When the duck is in the middle of the pond, fire a popper load and release your dog, telling him to *search* or *fetch*. Your dog will eagerly jump in the water and swim after the duck. Since the duck has a head start, your dog will have to work to catch him. The duck might dive or go into the cattails to hide. This is exactly what you want to happen. The duck's evasive actions will increase your dog's excitement and his desire to catch the duck. If the duck is really evasive, you might have to shoot him for your dog. Just be careful and only shoot the duck when there is no chance of hitting your dog. You want your dog to be successful in catching the duck. This is his reward. Now that your dog knows the drill and associates the firing of the gun and the command to search, you can have the next duck put out into the water with your dog out of sight. You and your dog stay out of sight of the pond. Have your helper toss the duck into the water. He can use rocks to throw behind the bird to get it to swim away from the shore and into cover. When the duck is no longer visible, the helper will call you and tell you to bring your dog up to the water. Take your dog on a lead with your shotgun and popper loads. Bring him to the water's edge, take off his lead, and fire your gun into the air. Give him the same search command. Your dog has been conditioned by you to go into the water and search for the duck when you fire your gun and release him. The scenario is the same except that he has not seen the bird. Your dog will go into the water and start to search for the duck. When he picks up the duck's scent he will follow it and attempt to retrieve it. If your dog has trouble picking up the scent or finding the duck, you can help him by putting out more than one duck. You can also start this phase of the training by using a smaller pond where the duck will be more confined. At the final stages of training, you can use larger water and let your dog expand his search. During your dog's search, stand by the water and do not give your dog any commands. Let him learn on his own where the bird is hiding. You want him to use his nose and desire to find the bird.

This final training in searching for a duck that the dog has not seen is very similar to the duck search in the Utility Test for NAVHDA. It is amazing to see a dog go into the water on command, search on his own for a wounded bird, find it, and retrieve it to hand. This is the mark of a true brag dog.

Finishing Touches:
Healing, Steadiness by Blind, Honoring Point

As we discussed in previous chapters, whoa training is the foundation for putting any other controls on your pointing dog. Once your dog is completely whoa trained and steady to wing, shot, and fall, then teaching him to heal, steadiness by blind, and honoring point is much easier. We will apply the same principles as we did when we taught the dog to whoa. We will also use the e-collar for all of these training sessions.

There are many times when it is important to have your dog under control when you are walking. You don't want your dog running amuck with other dogs around. In hunting situations, especially when I am jump-shooting ducks, I want my dog walking by my side. If he is running out in front of me he will be jumping ducks out of range.

Start your training by putting the e-collar on your dog and snapping a loose lead on him. I like to carry a double-barreled shotgun that is broken open. I want my dog to know this is a hunting situation. Stand beside your dog and start off walking slowly. When you take your first step, tell your dog to *heel*. Your dog will start to walk with you. Whenever he starts to get ahead, or pulls on the lead, give a short tug on the lead and hit the e-collar at the lowest level, at the same time give the verbal *heel* command. It probably will take several sessions until your dog figures out that he must walk slowly alongside you. When your dog is walking properly, praise him. Tell him he is a good

It may take some time for your dog to heel, but it will be well worth it.

The dog should always hold at the blind until you give him a release command.

boy. He soon will make the connection that he is doing the right thing when he walks with you. When you are finished heeling your dog, stop him with a *whoa* command. Then take the collar off and give him a release command. That tells him that it is all right to go. If you just let your dog loose without stopping him first, it will be harder for you to enforce heeling. Your dog will be constantly anticipating the release.

In order to hunt waterfowl successfully, your dog must be under control and be steady by the blind or in the boat. Steadiness by the blind is simply another form of whoa training. Your dog has learned that when he makes bird contact in the field he must stop and point and hold steady until you get to him, flush, and shoot the bird. Now you will teach your dog to be steady by the blind while the ducks are approaching, and also while you shoot. You will teach him to be steady until you give him a release command to go fetch the bird.

It's easier to use an assistant when teaching this command. Put the e-collar on your dog, snap a lead on him, and heel him to the water. Carry a shotgun that is broken open and some popper loads. When you get to the water, stop your dog and set him up. You want him to be facing the water. It is not important whether he lies down or sits. Give the dog a *whoa* command. Have your assistant hold the e-collar's transmitter and stand near the dog. Tell your assistant to hit the e-collar with a low stimulation and tone if the dog tries to leave the area. You should go about fifteen feet away and fire two shots in the air about ten seconds apart. Don't be concerned if your dog goes from a sitting to a standing position; as long as he stays where you placed him. If he tries to leave the area with these shots, have your assistant hit the low button on the e-collar. You can also use a verbal *whoa* command to stop him. When the dog will stay steady for two shots, go back to him and praise him. In each session, increase your distance from the dog, up to about twenty-five yards. If he remains still at that distance, go behind some trees or bushes to fire. At this stage your dog is tempted to go to you because he can't see you. Stop him with the e-collar. When he is totally steady during this stage, it is time to introduce another gunner, and a bird for your dog to retrieve.

Put out a few decoys in the water in front of the dog, leaving room for him to swim through them. Have your assistant take a gun and go about twenty-five yards and hide. You will stay by your dog with another gun. You will also have a dead duck that is out of sight of your dog. Have your assistant fire one shot, and then you fire a shot, followed by another shot from your assistant. As soon as your assistant fires his second shot, throw the duck in the water and fire a final shot in the air. If at any time your dog breaks, whoa him with a command and the e-collar. When the bird hits the water, give your dog the release command and have him fetch the bird. This sequence mirrors an actual duck-hunting scenario. Now your dog has learned to be steady while both you and other hunters shoot at birds. He knows to be steady by the blind until you give him a release command. During an actual hunting scenario, when ducks are flying in the air, your dog might be tempted to move. I like to have a couple of practice sessions in a blind with ducks flying and shooting before I take the e-collar off. For safety purposes, I will not send my dog for a retrieve with the collar on.

The finishing touch is teaching your dog to honor point. Honoring is extremely important if you are hunting two dogs, especially if one of the dogs belongs to your hunting partner. I have seen fights break out between dogs when one dog tries to steal another dog's point. Your hunting partner will also not be happy if your dog moves ahead of his and steals the point.

You can teach honoring with a dog cutout or with another dog. Personally, I like to use another dog. This is a good opportunity for you and your hunting partner to teach both of your dogs to honor each other. Plant a bird in the field and put e-collars on both dogs, making sure that the collars are on different frequencies, so that the wrong dog does not receive a stimulation. Have your partner release his dog and, when he gets close to the bird but before he points it, you release your dog. Make sure the first dog points the bird. When he does, your dog should stop and point when he sees the other dog on point. If he does not, stop him with the e-collar. Let the other handler flush the bird. Stand next to your dog and keep him on whoa. Praise him for not breaking.

Your dog has already been whoa trained and steady when making bird contact. Now you are teaching him that you want him to stop and point whenever he sees another dog on point. This is just a refinement of whoa training. Your dog will soon learn that when he sees another dog on point there is a bird there. You can alternate both dogs letting one find the bird and point it while the other backs. During the final phase of training, shoot the bird and alternate which dog gets the retrieve. This not only teaches the dogs to honor points but also reinforces steadiness.

If you do not have another dog that is totally steady, you can use a silhouette of a dog on point. You can make a simple one out of plywood. Put a hook on the top of the dog's head and attach a rope to the hook. You can use the rope to pull the dog up into pointing position. You can also buy a dog silhouette from the company from which you bought your e-collar. Their unit will work off of your e-collar transmitter. You can raise or lower the dog from a distance. This unit is great when you are training by yourself with no help.

Backing can be taught with either a wooden cutout, or with another dog.

How to Develop a Slow-starting Dog

Not all bird dogs develop their hunting abilities on the same timetable. The exceptional puppy will be a fast starter. You will look in amazement at how quickly he catches on. A fast-developing pup will start expanding his search and start finding and pointing birds at an early age; some as young as four to five months. If you have had pups that are early starters then you are lucky. Your job is much easier and your pup will develop his hunting skills faster. Many dogs will develop much more slowly. Just because they are not fast starters does not mean that they will not be great hunting dogs when they mature.

A number of years ago I kept two puppies from one of our litters: a male I named Duke and a female named Annie. They were born in the spring and I started hunting them on wild birds in the fall. Annie was a fast starter; she quickly learned how to find birds. She had an intense point and was a natural retriever. Duke was far more tentative in the bird field. He did not range out as far and he did not find as many birds as his sister. He had a solid point but not one that would get you excited. Because Annie was so exciting to watch and found more birds than Duke, she got more hunting time. Soon I was hunting her 75% of the time and Duke only 25%.

Late that fall, Blanche and I took Annie and her father, Baron, down to South Carolina for a quail hunt. We left Duke at home. Baron had gotten an infection in his foot and we were not able to hunt him. Annie, at eight months, got all of the hunting. The plantation we hunted had a number of big coveys of birds. Annie found six to eight coveys a day. She held her point until we flushed the covey and then retrieved the dead birds. We also hunted the singles after the covey rise. Annie was the star of the trip, with over fifty quail shot over her.

When we got home I continued to give Annie the lion's share of the hunting time. I started to become disappointed with Duke and I was about to give up on him. I was making an unfair comparison between Duke and his sister. Duke never got the time he needed and he actually should have had more time to develop than Annie. I mentioned to Blanche that I was thinking of selling Duke. Blanche suggested that before I made this decision, I should take Duke out and hunt him by himself and leave Annie at home.

The next morning Duke and I went hunting. Duke started out and slowly covered the field. In the first hour he found two pheasants. He held his point, I shot the birds, and Duke retrieved them. The third pheasant Duke found I managed to wing and the bird flew into the next bird field. Duke could not see where the bird landed but he ran across the field after the bird. I still had doubts about his ability, so I didn't follow him. I figured he would give up the hunt and would be back in a few minutes. After ten minutes I called him. He did not return. I started walking toward the other field, when I spotted Duke trotting toward me about one hundred yards out with the pheasant in his mouth. He retrieved it to hand, wagging his tail as I praised him. For the rest of the season I made sure that Duke got a great deal of hunting time. Now that he

Hunting Duke by himself allowed him to develope into a fine gun dog.

was getting to hunt more, I could see the excitement in him grow. His hunting ability improved with every outing. It was like seeing the light go on in his head. His development was just later than Annie's. I kept Duke, and he turned out to be a fine hunting dog. I also learned an important lesson, that every dog develops on a different time table and that you have to adjust your expectations and training to each dog's individual development. In many cases, dogs develop slower due to their physical or mental ability. I find that male dogs tend to develop slower than females.

In working with your dog, keep this individual development in mind. Give your dog as much time in the field as possible. When you hunt him on wild birds, try to put him down in an area where you know there are plenty of birds. You want him to make as much bird contact as possible. If you are hunting a shooting preserve, make sure you put a number of birds out for him. Each bird contact will increase your dog's excitement and his hunting knowledge. Do not over control your dog in the field. Let him work on his own to find the birds. If you are constantly trying to control him, he will spend all of his time watching you and waiting for your commands. He will never develop the confidence to hunt. Take your time in the bird field. When your dog finds and points a bird, make your best effort to kill the bird. If he flushes the bird, do not punish him. Every time your dog finds a bird for you and you have an opportunity to shoot it, make sure that you give your dog lavish praise. You want to convey to him that he is doing the right thing and that you are really happy with his performance.

Make sure that you work your dog by himself. Many slow-starting dogs are held back because they are hunted with an older dog or a sibling that has more drive and natural ability. This will only make the problem worse. The slower dog will hang back and defer to the other dog. Without attention and individual time, the slower dog may give up hunting. There is no incentive for him to hunt when the other dog gets all the birds and all the praise.

Your dog will probably work the bird field slowly at first. Be patient, you might not see improvement right away. However, you should see some slight improvement after three or four hunting sessions. As your dog gains more confidence and his desire increases so will his performance.

There are two other reasons why your dog might appear to be a slow starter. If your dog hangs back and does not show enthusiasm for hunting, it might be because you have put too much pressure on him and have over-controlled him. If you have been constantly calling him back and restricting his range, using your whistle incessantly, and hitting him with the e-collar, then you could have a dog that is afraid to hunt. Your actions have taught him that if he goes out and starts too search he will be punished. Consequently he will stay close to you and his search will shut down. He will spend all of his time looking at you and worrying about making a mistake and being punished. If this is the case, take off the e-collar and keep quiet. Let him range out and hunt. Do not scold him for extending his range. If he bumps a bird, so what? You need to build his confidence and desire. Make sure that every time he goes hunting he has a fun experience. It probably will take a number of hunting sessions before your dog recovers from his fear of punishment. He will spend time looking back at you for approval. When he does, it is best to keep quiet. He should turn back and start hunting again. An occasional *good boy* with a soft voice will also reassure him that he is doing okay.

A dog that has not been properly introduced to the gun, and has had too many shots fired over him at a young age, will also hang back. This is a case of a gun-sensitive dog or, worse yet, a dog that is gun shy. This is a very difficult problem and in many cases impossible to overcome. Try hunting your dog without a gun. If he starts to range out, praise him. Let him find birds. When he points a bird, go in quietly, flush the bird, and let him chase it. Each time he makes bird contact and does not hear the sound of the gun, he will start to overcome his fear. When he is boldly going out into the field and hunting, take a small blank pistol with you. Keep it in your pocket and do not let the dog see it. When you flush the bird let him chase it. When he is out at least forty to fifty yards chasing the bird, fire the gun one time. Use crimps because they make the least noise. Watch your dog and see how he reacts to the sound. If he pays no attention to it, you are on your way to curing the problem. If he has a reaction, do not fire the gun again until he has had several more bird contacts. If he pays no attention to the gun, then fire it every time he makes bird contact and is chasing the bird. When you are sure he is not at all affected by the sound of the blank gun, start carrying your shotgun with popper loads. The next time he makes contact with a bird and is chasing it, fire a popper load with your shotgun. You probably will need a whole season of gradually getting your dog used to the sound of a gun before you can start shooting birds over him. Hopefully, you will never encounter this problem.

Conditioning Your Dog for the Upcoming Hunting Season

Several years ago I was hunting with a friend and his English setter, Max. It was early in the season and the cover was thick and the temperature was hot. Max charged out into the field, located a pheasant, flash pointed, and then took the bird out. Pat yelled at Max. Max ignored him and flushed two more pheasants. It took Max a half hour to calm down. He finally held point on a bird and was steady to shot. By that time the heat had gotten to Max and we had to quit hunting him. It was obvious that he was not in good shape. I asked Pat if he had worked with Max during the summer. Pat said he hadn't been able to find the time. He told me that the last time Max had any bird contact or any physical workout was last fall during hunting season. The dog had been kept in his kennel for the last ten months. Max was a good dog with a good nose and great hunting potential. However, he never reached that potential because his owner didn't have time to spend in training and conditioning his dog.

A bird dog is like a professional athlete. He needs practice and conditioning to be in shape and to be able to perform like a pro. Every professional sport has a training camp where the athletes start months before the regular season. The purpose of the training camp is to get the players in top physical condition and to hone their playing skills. Most professional athletes have their own year-round training and conditioning program.

When you see other bird hunters out in the field, you can soon tell which hunters and their dogs are in good condition and producing birds. You can also tell which hunters and dogs have had no pre-season workouts. You can tell them best by the shouting that comes from the hunter yelling at his dog, "Whoa", " Whoa", "Stop", "@#%$&!" Bird hunting with a bird dog is a team sport. You and your dog work as a team to produce birds. The dog finds the bird, points it, and is steady holding the bird for you to get to him. Then it's your turn to flush the bird and shoot it. The ball then passes back to your dog as you release him and he goes out and finds the bird and retrieves it back to you. A great hunting team is a thing of beauty to watch. It is also an exhilarating experience for the hunter. To improve your bird hunting this coming year, start a weekly conditioning and training program now.

We try to follow a yearly training program with our dogs. In the winter months, we run our dogs once a week. Every Sunday morning, Blanche and I go out to a section of state game land with our German wirehaired pointers. We start our session with a half hour of letting the dogs run so that they get a chance to burn off their pent-up energy. The half hour run also keeps the dogs in good physical condition. When a day of hunting results in four to ten miles of foot travel for the hunter, the dog will travel four to six times as far. A hard-working hunting dog can easily cover fifteen to twenty miles or more in a day's hunt. Our dogs run hard during their Sunday morning workout. You can also road your dog with a bike or a four-wheeler. Pick the method that works best for you and your dog. You might want to vary the time you run your dog. Some dogs will require more time to stay in shape. Walking or riding a bike with your dog also helps you maintain your physical condition.

Starting in April and continuing throughout the summer, we expand our program to two days a week. Now that the weather is better, we expand our program to three parts. The first part is the half hour of conditioning and running. The second part is upland bird training and the third part is waterwork and conditioning.

In order to get the most out of your program, set up goals for each dog. Go over your dog's performance during the last hunting season. In what areas was he weak, and what areas need improvement? For your program, make a list of the things that you want to work on with your dog and plan out a systematic training session. Remember, you have all summer to work with your pup. Don't rush the training.

In addition to working on the specific areas that we want to improve with each dog, we make sure that every dog gets some bird work during each session. We use both pigeons and quail for our bird training. You can keep both birds year around at a nominal cost. There are a number of people who raise quail. Your local bird dog club can help you find a source for quail. There are a number of people who raise pigeons. Pigeon racing is a great sport and most areas have a club. They are also prolific birds. Most breeders are happy to give you their extra pigeons. We start our upland training sessions by putting all of our dogs on the chain gang. We want our dogs to be able to watch us training. This builds the dogs' enthusiasm and they can hardly wait for their turn in the field. Get together with your hunting buddies and help each other train. You can take turns planting birds and shooting for the person who is working his or her dog.

I like to plant two birds for each dog. That gives each dog about 15 minutes in the field. You can always plant more birds, or bring a dog back later for another short session. Our field session takes about an hour and a half for our four dogs. After the fieldwork, we go to a nearby lake for the water session.

We put all of our dogs back on the chain gang close to the water. Our dogs love the water and can't wait for their turn. We start with a play session for each dog. We throw a dummy into the water and have the dog retrieve it. We give each dog five or six retrieves and then we start the cycle all over again. This time we lead the dog up to the water, whoa him, and make him stay by our side while we throw the dummy. We give him the release command and have him retrieve the dummy to hand. We also use the dummy launcher for longer retrieves. We do the water last so that our dogs get a chance to cool down after the fieldwork.

The waterwork is a great way to help keep your dog in top condition. Swimming exercises all of the dog's muscles. Duke loved the water. He did not want to quit. He was in great shape and still was able to hunt hard for an hour or two every day up until he turned ten years old. I attribute this in large part to our year-round conditioning program and his love of the waterwork he got every summer. At ten he developed bone spurs on his spine. We had them removed surgically. However, they grew back. Duke found it difficult to run, especially on uneven ground. He still was able to swim and, up until the end, he loved the water.

Blanche and I and our dogs enjoy the training sessions. The dogs look forward to getting out each week for exercise and bird work. We have also noticed a marked improvement in their hunting ability in the fall. One other benefit is their increased health and endurance. We feel that the time we spend pays us back with huge dividends during hunting season. We have better-trained dogs and find more birds because of this training program.

First Aid Essentials in the Field

When you are hunting with your dog it is not a question of, will you need to give medical aid to your dog, but when and how often. Most instances are not life threatening but if not taken care of, it might end your hunt for the day. Cuts, cheat grass in the eye or ear, a tangle with a porcupine, cactus in a dog's paw; all of these incidents can occur, so you need to plan for them and have the proper tools to take care of your dog.

First and foremost, you need to have plenty of water. If you cover five miles a day hunting, your dog will cover two and a half times as much ground. That means your dog will run twelve miles to your five. He will need water in the field and also when he gets back to the truck. I carry ten gallons of water in my truck. I also carry one or two quarts of water in a soft plastic bottle in my hunting vest. In the back of my vest I carry a canvas collapsible water bowl. It weighs very little and folds up flat. It will hold a quart of water. During hot weather, your dogs should be watered and rested every ten to fifteen minutes.

I carry a pair of hemostats in my vest and I have another pair in my dog first aid box in my rig. I use the hemostats to pull porky quills out of my dogs, and to pull cactus out of their paws. I carry a complete dog first aid kit in my car. You can find a list of the essential items to carry in *A Field Guide to Dog First Aid*, written by Randy Acker DVM. Randy is an outstanding vet who hunts and specializes in sports medicine for dogs. His book is absolutely essential. I carry one in my first aid box and another one in my truck. Randy covers all of the problems that your dog can encounter in the field and how to give him emergency first aid. This book has saved the life of many a dog. Check the back of this book for a list of dog supply retailers where you can order it.

I carry dog pads and towels to dry my dogs when they get wet and cold. I also carry high-energy snacks for them, as well as some extra dog food, in case we get stuck out in the field overnight. At the end of each dog's hunt, put them up on your tailgate and check them over. Look at their paws for any cuts or thorns. Check their eyes and ears for any cuts or foreign objects and go over their entire body to be sure they do not have a problem. Most dogs will not indicate that there is a problem, especially when they are tired and happy after a day's hunt.

Check your dogs ears and eyes.

Removing a cactus from the dogs foot.

Hunting the Older Dog

When I first started writing for *Pointing Dog Journal* in the fall of 1996, Dave Meisner asked me to send him a photo of myself for the head of the article. The photo I sent in was of me and Duke, my German wirehaired pointer and my best hunting buddy for twelve years. Duke had hunted birds up to the end of his life, when he passed away from old age. However, during the last two years of his life, I learned how to adjust my hunting so that Duke could still participate without pain. I learned a great deal about how to hunt and take care of a dog as he ages. All dogs' lives are way too short. It is important to all of us who love dogs to spend as many years hunting with our canine pal as possible. When one of my customers learned that Duke had passed away, he sent me this short note.

> *"I'm sorry to hear about the loss of your best buddy, Duke. God played a cruel joke on man when he made dog's lifespan so short. My own best buddy, my Vizsla Mongo, enjoys hunting, camping, backpacking, hiking and fishing, and yes, he points trout. He's ten now and really hasn't slowed down much. But soon, I know... All the best, Paul Smith."*

It seemed like only yesterday that Duke was born into my hands. He was our constant companion. He went to the office with us each day; slept in the house; loved to hunt and also liked to go fishing with us. Duke was a strong, healthy dog. He hunted well with no noticeable slow down until his tenth year. That fall Duke was still able to hunt hard but he moderated his pace. I began to notice that he was slower getting up in the morning. He developed some stiffness in his hind legs. The spring of his eleventh year, Duke started to have serious problems getting up into the dog cap on the back of my pickup. Whenever, he had to go up or down a steep incline he had problems. An exam and x-rays taken by our vet, Connie VanLuchene, revealed that Duke had developed bone spurs on his discs. When his spine flexed, these bone spurs were hitting the spinal column and cutting off his circulation and the nerves that traveled to his hind legs. He was obviously uncomfortable. Duke also had arthritis. Connie started him on Rimydal, an arthritis medicine. She also suggested that I see a specialist veterinarian in Billings, Ed Moore. An exam by Ed confirmed the bone spurs and arthritis. He suggested surgery to remove the spurs. Ed was candid. While he could remove the spurs they would soon grow back. Nothing he could do would stop this aging problem. However, he felt this would give Duke several more years of a fairly active life. I decided to go ahead with the surgery.

Hunting season starts in Montana on September 1 for prairie birds. I hunted Duke opening day. He was still recovering from surgery, but you could tell by the bright look in his eyes and the thump of his tail on the floor as he watched me load the hunting gear in our truck that he still had the desire and eagerness to hunt. Now Duke rode in the back seat of our extended cab, not in the truck cap. We have four dogs, and like to rotate hunting them. We now made sure that we hunted Duke first. The mornings were much cooler and easier on him. During September, Duke would stop and lay down every ten minutes to rest. He had still not completely recovered from his surgery. In the beginning when he laid down I thought he was finished hunting for the day. I was wrong. He just needed some rest time. By mid-October and the start of pheasant hunting season, Duke had recovered much of his strength and was hunting longer periods. He had slowed down considerably, but his nose was as sharp as ever and he still found a great number of birds. Montana has varied terrain, with many hills and coulees that are quite steep. There is also a great deal of CRP land that is fairly level. I tried to hunt Duke in areas where the land was flat and fairly easygoing. He was a big dog, and plowing through thick cover was not a problem, but he still had problems going up and down steep inclines. Blanche and I had a great time hunting with Duke that fall. He got to hunt from an hour to an hour and a half. Then he was content to sit in the front seat of the truck while we hunted with our other wirehairs.

The next spring Duke's condition got worse. Another x-ray showed that the bone spurs were growing back rapidly. At twelve, I decided not to put him through another major operation. When hunting season rolled around that fall Duke was still eager to go. In the morning when I put on my hunting clothes he knew it was time to go hunting. He would go into the utility room and lay by the door to the garage waiting for me to put him in the truck. Now I had to lift him into the back seat. Our hunts were now limited to less than an hour. Duke tired very quickly. The spirit was willing but he physically couldn't handle more than a short hunt.

In October I took Chris VanLuchene, our vet's son, hunting with us. Chris was a teenager who had just gotten into hunting. This was his first bird hunt. It was also Duke's last hunt. We went to one of our favorite honey holes, a large flat area covered with sagebrush. There was a small creek with fresh cold water running through the middle of the land. The creek was perfect for keeping dogs cool in the hot sun. I knew where a large covey of sage grouse hung out. Duke slowly covered the ground. After ten minutes we started to see fresh bird droppings and Duke started getting birdy. He went on point and I called Chris over and told him to walk in front of Duke's point so he could flush the birds and shoot one. When Chris got in front of Duke, the birds exploded in the air. Chris was surprised and excited; he had never seen a sage grouse before. They looked like B-52 bombers taking off. Chris missed his first shot but knocked a bird down with his second barrel. The bird hit the ground and started to run. Duke loped past Chris, caught the bird and retrieved it to Chris. We took pictures of a proud young man holding his first wild bird with Duke at his side. I put Duke up and hunted my young dog Chukar for the rest of the morning.

Unfortunately, Duke was not able to hunt any more that fall. During the holidays, Connie came to the house and, with Duke in my arms, put him gently to sleep. Duke was born into my hands and passed away in my arms, a great companion and hunting buddy. All of our dogs are an integral part of our lives. When they pass away we have them cremated and place the boxes on the mantle over our fireplace in our bedroom. They will be buried with us when we pass away.

From my experience with Duke, I learned a great deal about how to take care of and enhance an older dog's life and hunting ability. Not long after this experience, I received a call from Chuck Moxley, an old friend of mine who was also our vet when we lived in Ohio. During the conversation the subject of hunting and caring for the aging dog came up. Chuck is an avid hunter and cares for a number of hunting dogs in his clinic. I told him I wanted to write an article to help other hunters take care of their older hunting dogs. Together, we came up with the following recommendations.

Hunting dogs are professional athletes like Roger Clemens, Nolan Ryan, and Carl Malone. We all revere these older athletes not only for their dominating performances but also for their longevity. We ask no less of our gun dogs. They must perform at a very high level, with a great deal of energy, in tough terrain and all kinds of weather. In order to do this, you need to provide them with the following things to help their performance.

Diet: In this day and age there is no excuse to feed performance gun dogs a budget dog food. There are a number of companies that make premium dog foods that have the necessary ingredients, vitamins, and trace minerals that your dog needs. There is a great deal of difference in the type of protein used by the premium dog food companies and the budget dog food firms. Your dog's performance in the field will only be as good as the fuel you give him. I feed my dogs a performance formula during the entire hunting season. During the rest of the year, I feed the same formula, but cut back on the amount each dog receives, based on its off-season activity. You can feed a good maintenance formula also, but I find my dogs are more eager to eat their meals if they receive the performance formula.

Conditioning and Training: Championship athletes don't get in and out of shape. Today's sports stars are in continuous training, and they stay in shape all year long. Your hunting dog needs the same type of year-round conditioning. I run my dogs several times a week all year long. One of the best exercises for a dog, especially an older dog, is swimming. Swimming works all of a dog's muscles. It also helps his aerobic conditioning. The great advantage with swimming is that there is no stress or pounding on the dog's legs and muscles. Duke loved to swim and retrieve dummies in the water. He was able to go swimming without pain until the very end.

Preventive Medicine: Make sure your dog has a thorough annual exam, along with blood work and a urinalysis. This will help identify problems in their early stages, when they are easier to deal with and treat. Be watchful, and communicate with your veterinarian about early signs of arthritis and other signs of physical problems. Make sure you use a vet that understands the physical demands that are required of your dog and has an intense interest in sports veterinary medicine.

Chuck Moxley has found that a daily dose of glucosamine and chondroitin helps lubricate a dog's joints. I have an arthritis problem with my fingers. Since I have started taking glucosamine and chondroitin, my condition has improved. With the results I experienced, I decided to give my older dogs this same nutrient when they reach eight years of age. Many of the dog catalogs sell this in a formula developed specifically for dogs.

Adjust and moderate your hunting day to accommodate your older dog. We all have honey holes where we know there are birds. By letting your older dog hunt these small areas, you can both have a great hunting experience without tiring him. I have also changed hunting rigs. I now have a four-door pickup with my dog box on the back of the truck. When any of my dogs gets too old to get up into the dog box, I let them ride in the back of the cab. I have a short ramp that will make it easy for my older dogs to get into the cab.

Losing your hunting buddy can be a very difficult and often depressing situation. I have found getting a puppy when your dog gets older can help both you and your older dog. A young playful pup will often bring renewed energy to the older dog and it also helps ease the pain and the sorrow when you lose that special buddy.

I hope this helps all of you enjoy as many years as possible with your hunting dogs.

The Quail Pen:
It Takes Birds to Make a Bird Dog

Athletes who are good at their game, like Tiger Woods and Phil Mickelson, spend more time hitting balls on the practice range than they do in actual competition. They also spend more time training than the other pros. The same principle holds true in training pointing dogs. If you want to have an outstanding bird dog, make sure that he gets a lot of actual live bird contact. Your dog will be working wild birds during the hunting season, however most seasons last for only two or three months in the fall. You can extend your season by visiting your local shooting preserve during the winter, but most preserve seasons end in March. That leaves the crucial months of April through August or September without a wild bird or preserve season. These are the very months that it is most important to be working your dog on birds.

There is an economical solution to the problem. Most states have a dog-training season that will allow you to release and shoot birds during a training session. Check with your state fish and game department for the rules and regulations. As a rule, the state will require you to have a license or permit that will allow you to train your dog on birds. Normally they will require you to have a designated grounds or area where you intend to train. In many states they will allow you to train on state game land. If you have enough land or know someone who does, you are in good shape.

If you are looking for a place to train, how about checking with the farm or ranch where you have permission to hunt? NAVHDA – North American Versatile Hunting Dog Association – can be a big help in your search for training grounds. Check with NAVHDA and find out the nearest chapter in your area. Their chapters are very active in training. As a member, you can train with them and probably use their training ground. Another good source is the National Shoot to Retrieve Association. They have a number of local bird dog clubs that run shoot to retrieve trials. You can bet that the members who actively run their dogs in shoot-to-retrieve are constantly training. Again, check with your state fish and game department or your local outdoor editor of your newspaper for the local bird dog clubs. Whether you train with a club, or do it yourself on state game land or private land, you still need birds; and quail fit the bill perfectly.

A quail callback pen, often referred to as a Johnny house, is an economical way to keep quail for training purposes. You can build one in less than a day with a minimal amount of tools and for less than two hundred dollars. A small quail pen will hold up to twenty-four birds. The typical house is four feet by four feet by six feet high. The bottom part is made of ¾-inch exterior plywood. Above the plywood is a screened area made of ½-inch hardware cloth. There is a shelf around the top of the plywood where the birds can sit and sun themselves. One side of the top has a twenty-four-inch by twenty-four-inch door that opens out. This door enables you to reach in and catch quail. You can also open the door and let four or five birds fly out. The top of the pen is covered with galvanized steel. The roof is built on a slant so the water and snow will slide off. The bottom of the pen is a frame covered with ½-inch galvanized wire to allow the bird droppings to fall through. The wire also helps prevent predators from digging in and getting at your birds. The front side of the house has a small trap door that can be dropped down to use in recalling birds to the pen. When the door is open, the birds can re-enter the quail pen through the funnel. Attached to the front wall is a funnel made of the same wire mesh that you use for the floor. The funnel has an opening circle with a diameter of five inches. It is twelve inches long. The other opening inside the pen is only three inches in diameter. The smaller opening is to deter the quail from trying to escape. The end of the funnel inside the pen should be slanted up at least twelve inches from the floor. You want this opening to be above the head of the birds. If the birds can see the opening, they will try to enter and escape. I like to cut a piece of plywood about thirty inches long and thirty-six inches high and attach it inside the pen, on a slant against the side wall away from the funnel opening. This shelter allows the quail to get behind it to hide and to roost during the night. I live in Montana and have kept quail alive and healthy through a Montana winter where the temperatures often drop to twenty degrees below zero during the night. The quail pen protects the quail from the wind and snow and keeps their food dry. As long as you have enough quail to form a tight covey, normally eight to ten birds, they can generate enough heat to survive. I put a large door on the back of the pen. This door allows me to reach in and refill their feeder, water container, and grit pan. I also use this opening to catch quail. I located my Johnny house in my back yard. I have eight acres that I leave in native prairie grass. I use my yard to start all of my young puppies on birds. After the birds have been in the pen for several weeks, you can release some of them. Make sure that you keep at least one male in the pen, although I prefer to keep two or three males. The penned males will call back the released birds to the pen. I leave the trap door open and put some quail feed on the open door leading into the funnel. The released quail will covey back to the pen and enter through the door. In the morning, I close the door to make sure they do not get back out.

Now you have a quail pen and a supply of birds in your own yard that you can use for training. If your property is too small to train on, you can still keep the Johnny house there. If you must train elsewhere, buy a portable quail callback pen. This recall pen is a miniature version of the Johnny house. It is made of steel mesh and is about fifteen inches wide by thirty inches long by eight inches high with a funnel that lets quail back in the pen. You can use this portable pen to transport your birds to the training area. If you want to recapture your birds after training, make sure that you leave a male call bird in the pen. The birds will usually start to come back to the pen several hours after the training session ends.

You will need a plastic waterer, a grit pan, and a steel feeder for your pen. I find that I need to check the pen and fill up the feeder and give them fresh water on a weekly basis. However, during the heat of the summer, I give them fresh water twice a week. I give the birds new grit every other week. I also find that a small hand-held fishing net is very handy when I catch the quail for a training session.

Food, water, and grit containers.

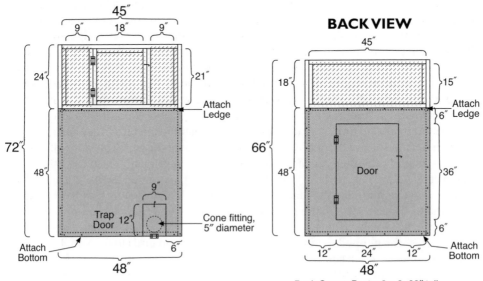

FRONT VIEW

Front Corner Posts: 2 × 2, 72″ tall

Mesh
Side Panels: 11″ wide × 23″ tall
Door Panel: 20″ wide × 21″ tall

Trap Door hinge attaches to inside of trap door and bottom (ground side) of floor. Use 1 latch.
Dimensions: 9″ wide by 12″ tall.

Top Door attaches with 2 hinges and 1 latch.
Dimensions: 21″ square.

BACK VIEW

Back Corner Posts: 2 × 2, 66″ tall

Mesh: 45″ wide × 17″ tall

Door attaches with two hinges and one latch.
Dimensions: 24″ wide by 36″ tall

LEDGE

Ledge, using 1 × 6 in specified lengths. Cut 1½″ notches in 48″ long boards to fit corner posts.

BOTTOM

Six (6) 2 × 2, 45″ long:
Four (4) posts spread between corner posts;
Two (2) spaced evenly between sides and attached to side posts.

© 2006 Wilderness Adventures Press, Inc.

QUAIL PEN PLANS

SIDE VIEW

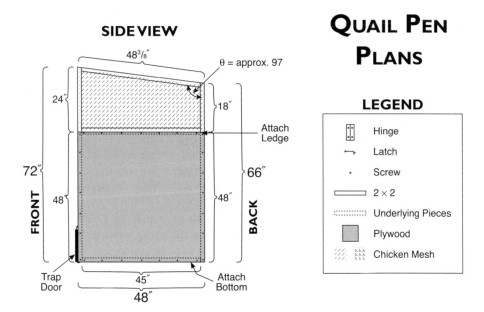

θ = approx. 97

48³⁄₈″

24″

18″

Attach Ledge

72″

66″

FRONT

48″

48″

BACK

Trap Door

45″

Attach Bottom

48″

LEGEND

Hinge	
Latch	
Screw	
2 × 2	
Underlying Pieces	
Plywood	
Chicken Mesh	

CUTAWAY VIEW

Showing roof dimensions, lean-to shelter, and how to attach cone

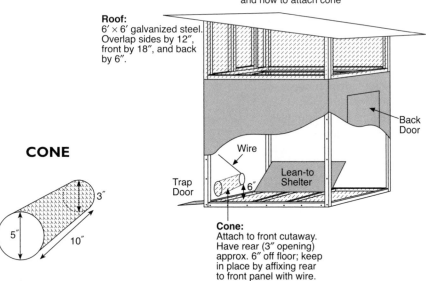

Roof:
6′ × 6′ galvanized steel. Overlap sides by 12″, front by 18″, and back by 6″.

Back Door

Wire

Lean-to Shelter

Trap Door

6″

CONE

5″

3″

10″

Cone:
Attach to front cutaway. Have rear (3″ opening) approx. 6″ off floor; keep in place by affixing rear to front panel with wire.

Cone, using a single pice of mesh approximately 16″ long by 10″ wide, rolled to the specified dimensions.

Now that you have your deluxe quail pen built, you are ready to order birds. Almost every state has a number of game bird breeders. In order to raise game birds commercially, you need a state license. When you contact your fish and game department for information on training with birds, ask them to provide you with a list of game bird breeders. Most breeders are members of the North American Game Bird Association. They have an excellent website that lists all of the members by state. See www.naga.org. You can also contact any of the field trial organizations in your area. You can't run a field trial, shoot-to-retrieve trial, or NAVHDA test without game birds. Most bird breeders have all of the business they can handle and they only raise a certain number of birds each year. It pays to contact them early and reserve your birds in advance. I usually order twenty-five quail for late August delivery when I know that I will be having a litter of puppies and will need quail for them, as well as my older dogs.

Quail are very reasonable in price. I am currently paying $3.50 a bird plus shipping. My breeder ships his birds via the post office. Shipping costs on twenty-five birds runs me less than $10.00. The post office will get your birds to you in one or two days. I have never lost a bird using the post office. They normally will call you and let you know when they arrive, but you might want to check with your post office in advance to let them know when you are expecting a shipment of live birds.

I feed my quail Purina Game Bird Flight Conditioner. It comes in fifty-pound bags and costs $8.75. The grit comes in a fifty-pound bag and costs $7.25. Following are material and equipment lists for the Johnny house:

MATERIAL LIST:
- Two four-foot sheets of ½-inch exterior plywood
- Four pieces of framing wood, six feet by 1½ inches
- Sixteen feet of ½-inch x two-inch wood for the shelf
- Five foot x five foot galvanized steel for the roof
- Thirty feet of ½-inch hardware cloth for the sides, floor, and funnel
- Wood screws
- Three latches for the doors
- Five hinges for doors

EQUIPMENT LIST:
- One plastic waterer: two-quart size
- One steel feeder
- One steel grit pan
- Portable recall pen, if training on a different location

You can build your Johnny house and buy all of the equipment for around $200.00. I built my house over ten years ago and it is still in good condition. During the spring and summer when I am working with young dogs, I often will use fifty to one hundred quail. Let's compare the costs with sending your dog to a professional trainer. A good pro will charge you $450.00 a month and up. They are worth every penny. For the same amount of money you can work your dogs over one hundred birds a year. I am not suggesting that you should not use a pro. However, if you have the time and enjoy training your bird dog, you can do it at a very reasonable cost. My dogs and I look forward to the summer and our twice-weekly training sessions. My pups are into birds all year and are ready to go the first day of September, when our season starts in Montana.

HERE IS A LIST OF SOURCES THAT YOU WILL FIND HANDY:
- Gun Dog Supply at www.gundogsupply.com
- Lion Country Supply at www.lcsupply.com or 1-800-662-5202
- Scott's Dog Supply at www.scottsdog.com or 1-800-966-3647

FOR GAME BREEDERS CONTACT:
- North American Game Bird Association at www.naga.org
- NAVHDA (North American Versatile Hunting Dog Association at www.navhda.org
- National Shoot to Retrieve at www.nstra.org

Chuck and Chukar

Pigeons:
The Ideal Bird for Dog Training

It takes birds to train and make a bird dog. When you start steadying your dog and whoa training him you will need a great many birds. The whoa training process can take from one to three months of training on a three times a week to daily basis. You whoa train a dog to stop and be steady when he makes bird contact. In order to do that, you must have birds for your training sessions. I normally use three to five pigeons for each dog during each training session. Let's figure it out. At three sessions a week, you will need a total of twelve birds. For a three-month period you will need about one hundred birds for each dog.

Pigeons are ideal birds to use for most of your whoa training. They are also great birds to use to teach your dog to retrieve. Pigeons are inexpensive to buy and to keep. The great thing about them is the same birds can be used over and over again. Pigeons can be taught to fly back to their roost. If you have a bird in a release trap and release it while you whoa your dog, the bird will fly back to the pen. The same bird can be used again for the next training session.

Okay, you're sold on the idea of getting and using pigeons. There are two ways to acquire them. You can buy a trap and trap them. My friend, Chris Francis, and I decided to train with pigeons. We built a pen and Chris, who trapped as a kid, said he had access to a couple of old barns that were loaded with birds. We bought a trap and Chris spent several weeks climbing the barn rafters loading the trap with food. After a couple of weeks of this, Chris and I realized the pigeons were winning. We finally gave up on that idea and decided to buy pigeons.

The best place to buy pigeons is from a pigeon breeder or a member of a pigeon club. There are hundreds of racing pigeon clubs in the U.S. Contact the American Racing Pigeon Union, Inc. 405-848-5801 or visit their web site www.warpu.org. They have a state-by-state listing of clubs. Pigeon racers and enthusiasts keep a number of birds. Breeders always have extra birds that they are willing to sell since pigeons, like rabbits, are frequent breeders. I bought twelve pigeons for $3.00 apiece. Before you buy your birds, you will need to build a loft and obtain some equipment and food for your birds.

Your loft should be able to house eighteen to twenty-four birds. (See the sidebar for the materials and blue print to build a small loft.) You will need a feeder that will hold grain for the birds as well as a grit pan. Pigeons need grit every day. For water, you will need a two-gallon water pail. If you are in a climate that dips below the freezing mark in winter, you will need to put the water fountain on a heater platform. I place an electric water heater under the platform. This is a simple heater that uses a twenty-five-watt light bulb to keep the water from freezing. The platform serves as a place for the birds to sit when they drink. You will need a bird crate to transport the birds to the training area and to train them to fly back to the pen. I use the same bird crate that I use to carry my pheasants and chukars. Food is easy to obtain. Most of the feed stores that sell dog food have pigeon food. Purina makes a pigeon feed, as do many other manufacturers. A fifty-pound bag of feed costs me $10.00. You will also need boxes for each pair of birds to nest. I use small plastic milk crates. I turn the crates sideways and stack them three high against the back wall of the pen. My small pen will hold nine crates enough to house nine pairs of pigeons.

Make sure that you buy young birds that are just starting to fly. You want your birds to home back to your loft. Older birds that have been flown will tend to return to the loft from which they came. Bring your birds home and put them in their loft. Keep them in the loft for two to three weeks without letting them out to fly. You want them to regard the loft as their home. After that time, you can open the loft door and let them out to fly each day. Before you let them fly for the first time, let them go without food for a couple of days. When you release your birds, fill up the food dish. The birds will be hungry and will come back to the loft to eat after a short time. In the first weeks after I started releasing my birds I had three birds leave and not return. The rest of the birds came back every day after flying. Now I leave the loft entrance open. My birds are free to come and go as they want. They spend a lot of time each day flying, returning every afternoon to feed and sleep. If I am going to train dogs and need birds, I shut the loft door the night before. The loft door has metal bobs that hang down the opening. The birds can push the bobs in to get into the loft. However, the bobs hang down below the bottom of the opening, so the birds cannot push their way out. The next day I go into the loft and catch the number of birds I need for my training session. If you are training in an area that is a distance from your loft, you will have to train your birds to return. This is a fairly simple process. Each week, as often as you have time, catch your birds and put them in the carrying crate. Take the birds down the road about a quarter of a mile and release them. They will fly back to the loft. Gradually increase the distance that you release the birds from the loft until you are letting them go where you do your regular dog training. When you get home you'll find that your pigeons have already returned to their pen.

Pigeons start breeding in the spring. Every pair of birds will have a hatch of from two to four birds. They will continue to hatch for several months. A group of twelve birds will provide you with enough young birds to train several dogs each year. Young birds are ready to fly in about two months.

Side 1 and front of the pigeon coop.

Side 2 of the pigeon coop.

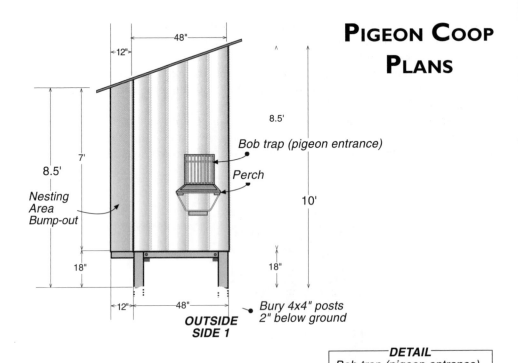

Pigeon Coop Plans

48"

12"

8.5'

Bob trap (pigeon entrance)

Perch

7'

8.5'

Nesting
Area
Bump-out

10'

18"

18"

12"   48"

Bury 4x4" posts
2" below ground

**OUTSIDE
SIDE 1**

DETAIL
Bob trap (pigeon entrance)

14¹/₂" x 17¹/₄"

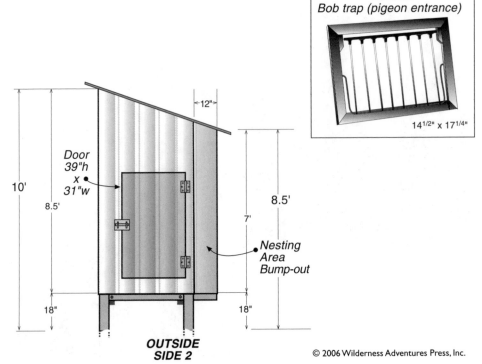

12"

Door
39"h
x
31"w

10'

8.5'

8.5'

7'

Nesting
Area
Bump-out

18"

18"

**OUTSIDE
SIDE 2**

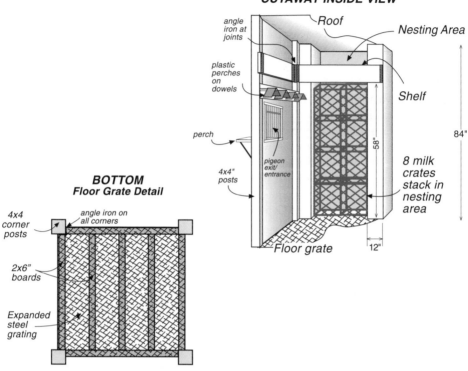

CUTAWAY INSIDE VIEW

Roof

Nesting Area

angle iron at joints

plastic perches on dowels

Shelf

perch

84"

58"

4x4" posts

pigeon exit/ entrance

8 milk crates stack in nesting area

Floor grate

12"

BOTTOM
Floor Grate Detail

4x4 corner posts

angle iron on all corners

2x6" boards

Expanded steel grating

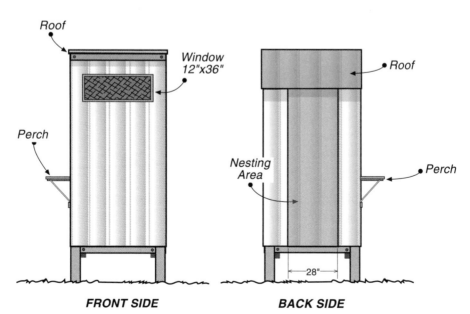

Roof

Window 12"x36"

Perch

FRONT SIDE

Roof

Nesting Area

Perch

28"

BACK SIDE

© 2006 Wilderness Adventures Press, Inc.

PIGEON COOP EQUIPMENT LIST:

- **Corner Posts:** (4) 4" x 4", 12'
- **Exterior Plywood:** (2) 4' x 8' - ¾"
- **Expanded Steel Grate Floor:** 4' x 4'
- **Bottom Frame:** 2 x 6's (attached with angle iron and brackets)
- **Pen:** Should sit 18" above ground to allow for raking droppings through grate
- **Ledge:** Above nesting area in back - 14" wide, also in front
- **Roof:** 10-degree slope front to back; 8" overhang in both front and back. Cover roof with ¾" exterior plywood, plus Delta ribbed-aluminum siding
- **Nesting Boxes:** 8 milk crates (12"w x 14"h x 10"d)
- **Coop:** Use Delta ribbed-aluminum siding over exterior plywood on sides and roof
- **Inside:** 2" dowels (to hold plastic perches)
- 2' x 4' brace above pigeon entrance
- 2' x 4' brace above door to hold 4 plastic perches

PURCHASE FROM PIGEON SUPPLIERS:

- pigeon bob trap doors
- waterer/water heater
- grit pan
- feeder
- plastic perches

FOLLOWING IS A LIST OF SOME SOURCES FOR PIGEON SUPPLIES:

Foy's Pigeon Supplies
3185 Bennetts Run Road
Beaver Falls, PA 15010
1-877-355-7727
They also have a catalog

Global Pigeon Supplies
2301 Rowland Ave
Savannah, GA 31404
1-800-562-2295
www.globalpigeon.com

Gun Dog Supply
www.gundogsupply.com
1-800-624-6378

Lion Country Supply
www.lcsupply.com
1-800-662-5202

All of these companies have catalogs and offer all of the equipment and supplies for pigeons, including books and videos.

Epilogue

For the past forty years, I have been a passionate bird dog man and bird hunter. Each season my excitement and passion for the hunt increases. I continue to find ways to increase the number of days I spend in the field with my dogs. I love watching my German wirehaired pointers glide through the fields and the excitement I see when they slam on point or when they leap in the air and into the water after a duck.

Throughout the year my thoughts are on the land, the birds, and the dogs... always the dogs.

Here's hoping that you have many great hunts with your versatile hunting dog.

Good Shots,
Chuck & Blanche Johnson

Appendix One:
Gun Dog Training Supplies

Gun Dog Supply
website, and a retail store in Mississippi
www.gundogsupply.com
1-800-624-6378

Lion Country Supply
catalog, website, and a store in
Pennsylvania
www.lcsupply.com
1-800-662-5202

Scott's Dog Supply
catalog, website, and a store in Indiana
www.scottsdog.com
1-800-966-3647

Bass Pro
web site, catalog, and retail stores across
the country
www.basspro.com
1-800-976-6344

Cabela's
website, catalog, and retail stores across
the country
www.cabelas.com
1-800-237-4444

Wilson D's Sporting Goods
catalog, and retail store
1-888-456-5150

Sportsman's Warehouse
website and retail stores across the
country
www.sportsmanswarehouse.com

Ugly Dog Hunting
website and catalog
www.uglydoghunting.com
1-877-982-7054

Versatile Dogs .Com
www.versatiledogs.com
This is a web site that has breed
descriptions, a kennel listing with litter
announcements and started dogs for
sale. They also have a dog club directory
and an events forum.

Pointing Dog Journal
Magazine, eight issues a year. For a
subscription call 800-447-7367.

FOR GAME BREEDERS CONTACT:
North American Game Bird Association
www.naga.org

Scotts Dog Supply kennel

Appendix Two:
Versatile Hunting Dog Associations

American Wirehaired Pointing Griffon Association
www.awpga.com
- This group has clubs across the country. They have a quarterly newsletter.

Large Munsterlander Club of North America
www.lmcna.org
- The club maintains a registry. Their website also lists upcoming litters and Large Munsterlander eligible breeders. They also have a quarterly newsletter.

NAVHDA - North American Versatile Hunting Dog Association
www.navhda.org
1-847-253-6488
- This is the premier organization for all the versatile breeds. They maintain a registry and they have over 5,000 members across the country in a number of chapters. They also have a great testing program. With your membership you receive a monthly magazine. Their website lists upcoming tests and events. I urge every versatile dog owner to belong to this great group. There is a membership application in this section of the book.

National Shoot to Retrieve
www.nstra.org
- Organized field trials, and field trial registry. Organized into regional chapters.

North American Deutsch Kurzhaar Club
www.nadkc.org
- The Kurzhaar is the German-bred shorthair. This organization has regional clubs around the country. They have a testing and a breeding program. They also have a registry. Their web site lists available litters and Kurzhaar kennels along with upcoming tests.

North American Pudelpointer Alliance
www.pudelpointer.org
- This organization uses the NAVHDA testing system. Their web site lists breeders.

The Pudelpointer Club of North America
www.pcna.org
- The Pudelpointer club has chapters around the country. They have their own testing program and a breed improvement test along with a registry. Contact information is on their website.

Small Munsterlander Club of North America
www.smallmunsterlander.org
- The club encourages the testing of their breed in the NAVHDA system. Their website has litter announcements.

Spinone Club of America
www.spinone.com
- Their website has a litter registry and a list of reputable breeders.

Verein Deutsch Drahthaar - Group North American
www.vdd-gna.org
- The VDD is the German-bred wirehaired pointer. The VDD has a testing program, a breeding program, and a registry. They have chapters around the country. Their website lists upcoming litters and VDD kennels, along with their test calendar.

Wirehaired Pointing Griffon Club of America
www.wpgca.org
- This group has regional chapters. They have a testing and breeding program. Their website lists their test dates.

German Wirehaired Pointer Club of America
www.gwpca.com

German Shorthaired Pointer Club of America
www.gspca.org

Vizsla Club of America
http://clubs.akc.org/vizsla

Weimaraner Club of Americaa
www.weimclubamerica.org

National Red Setter Field Trial Club
www.nrsftc.com
- The Red Setter club website includes breed, standards, breeders, dogs at stud and upcoming litters. They also show upcoming trials and events.

Dog Kennel Plans

By Dennis Nelson

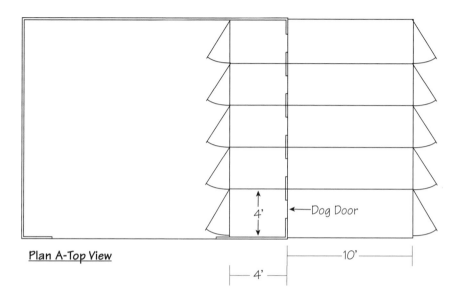

Plan A-Top View

4'

←—Dog Door

10'

4'

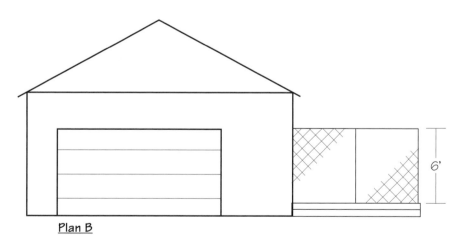

Plan B

6'

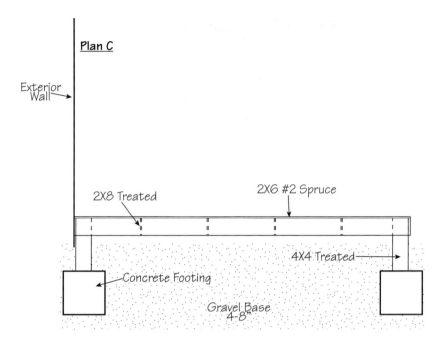

Plan C

Exterior Wall

2X8 Treated

2X6 #2 Spruce

4X4 Treated

Concrete Footing

Gravel Base 4-8"

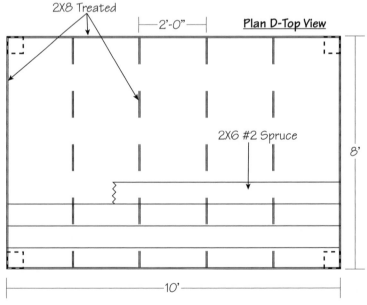

2X8 Treated

2'-0"

Plan D-Top View

2X6 #2 Spruce

8'

10'

NAVHDA INTERNATIONAL MEMBERSHIP APPLICATION

Mail to: NAVHDA, P.O. Box 520, Arlington Heights, IL 60006
Overseas Membership: for shipping and postal costs, add $30.00 to listed membership fee.

To pay by credit card:
include Credit Card Information with this application and check this box: ☐

Make checks payable in U.S. funds to NAVHDA.

Dues are tax deductible in U.S.
(Tax# 95-3402489 under 501(c)(3) as an Educational Corporation)

CHOOSE THE MEMBERSHIP PACKAGE THAT BEST SUITS YOUR NEEDS:
All memberships include our monthly magazine

☐ $50.00 New Membership
New Member Packet including
NAVHDA Aims, Programs, Test Rules
book and decal.

☐ $73.50 New Member Package
(IL residents add $5.82 tax) Includes the
NAVHDA Training Book ($15.50 Value)
and the 60 minute correlating Training
DVD ($28.95 Value), NAVHDA Aims,
Programs, Test Rules book, and decal.

☐ $45.00 Renewal Regular Membership

☐ $22.50 Spouse Membership

☐ $22.50 Junior Membership
(up to 16 yrs.)

☐ $1000.00 Life Membership Endowment

☐ $175.00 Down Payment on Life Membership Endowment Installment Plan

Name _____
Given Name and Initials

Street _____

City_____ State/Province _____ Postal Code_____

Phone _____-_____-_____ E-mail _____

Please tell us about yourself and your involvement with versatile hunting dogs:

Name_____

Daytime Phone# _____-_____

☐ MasterCard   ☐ VISA   ☐ Other _____

Credit Card# __ __ __ __ - __ __ __ __ - __ __ __ __ - __ __ __ __

Expiration Date __ __ - __ __

Signature _____ Date_____